P9-BJQ-955

Ferrum College

FOR USE IN

Stanley Library

THE PUBLISHERS

ABINGDON PRESS

DISCARDED
BY
STANLEY LIBRARY
FERRUM COLLEGE

(continued from front flap)

hit a dry spell? How does group prayer life provide new dimensions of growth?

For those who recognize the need for change, who seek the freedom found through prayer, who want to pray and to grow, this perceptive book is a creative beginning.

FLORA SLOSSON WUELLNER'S special interest in the subject of prayer has led her to continuing research, study, and teaching. Now a homemaker and writer, she lives in Berkeley, California, with her husband Wilhelm, professor of New Testament at Pacific School of Religion. They have three daughters.

Mrs. Wuellner received her B.A. and M.A. degrees from the University of Michigan and the B.D. degree from Chicago Theological Seminary.

Also by Flora Slosson Wuellner:
PRAYER AND THE LIVING CHRIST

This exciting approach to the practice of Christian prayer reinforces the fact that Christ is a living presence in the world today who can work through us if we accept the unique power he offers us through prayer.

TO PRAY AND TO GROW

TO PRAY AND TO GROW

flora slosson wuellner

Nashville   ABINGDON PRESS   New York

BV
210
.2
.W82

To Pray and to Grow

Copyright © 1970 by Abingdon Press

All rights in this book are reserved.
No part of the book may be reproduced in any
manner whatsoever without written permission of
the publishers except brief quotations embodied in
critical articles or reviews. For information address
Abingdon Press, Nashville, Tennessee.

ISBN 0-687-42293-0
Library of Congress Catalog Card Number: 70-124757

Scripture quotations unless otherwise noted are
from the Revised Standard Version of the Bible,
copyrighted 1946 and 1952 by the Division of
Christian Education, National Council of Churches,
and are used by permission.

SET UP, PRINTED, AND BOUND BY THE
PARTHENON PRESS, AT NASHVILLE,
TENNESSEE, UNITED STATES OF AMERICA

To My Father and Mother
Channels of God's Love

49877

STANLEY LIBRARY
FERRUM JUNIOR COLLEGE

CONTENTS

CAN CHRIST REALLY CHANGE ME?

We Christians have become bold—but also strangely timid. The boldness is obvious and breathtaking. We march in demonstrations for racial justice. We challenge war and we defy unjust laws—even to the point of going to prison. Our ministers take their guitars into the pulpit and quote Peanuts in their sermons. The creeds are openly debated, and the liturgies undergo experimental change. Priests and nuns claim new freedoms and wear the layman's dress. Theological students dance barefoot in the grass and share tea and cookies for Communion. There is growing interest in expressing worship through new depths of sensory awareness: color, taste, touch, and hearing. Young people and the unchurched are being listened to as never before. Old hypocrisies and masks are being cast aside.

It is becoming again, thank God, an adventurous, almost disreputable thing to be a Christian leader, much as it was in the early centuries of Christianity. The world no longer knows what to expect of us!

But there is also a strange and growing timidity. Increasingly we avoid the question of personal "holiness." We speak freely of what Christ does in *community*, how the force of his Spirit works on social and racial problems; but we are reluctant to discuss the radical changes he works on *individuals*. We talk a great deal about how he will eventually bring this world into his Kingdom, but very little is being said these days about how he can turn each one of us into a "new creation" on all levels.

The power of prayer, the meaning of guidance, the reality of the invisible dimensions around us, our growing awareness of the hand of Christ on our lives, the perception of deeper levels of beauty and union with God: these subjects are generally avoided in our churches, as once the subjects of racial prejudice, life in the slums, and economic injustice were avoided. We have new taboos now. A group discussion on sex no longer makes a Christian blush, and that is fine. But watch him go all modest and mumbling when asked about his prayer life!

10

The reasons for this shyness and reluctance are obvious. We are afraid that any such emphasis on personal change and growth in Christ will set us apart from other men and women. Then, too, the sanctimonious, self-righteous Christian is a repulsive object. I found an example of this in two hymns typical of what was sung in our Christian churches a century ago:

> What scenes of horror and of dread
> Await the sinner's dying bed . . .
> His sins in dreadful order rise,
> And fill his soul with sad surprise; . . .
>
> I see the pleasant bed
> Where lies the dying saint,
> Though in the icy arms of death
> He utters no complaint. . . .

Most of us are still reacting against these priggish, unrealistic images of "sinner" and "saint." For much too long Christians were encouraged to dwell with exclusive emphasis on personal sanctity, and far too often the wrong kind of sanctity.

These deeply embedded images of "holiness" are a real, though perhaps subconscious, stumbling block to our churches. We are trying to atone for our self-righteousness. We are trying to witness to our oneness with the rest of humanity. Our major emphasis and interest these days is the eager effort to reach out to the world, involve the church as a community, in living redemptively in other communities. We are more in-

11

terested than we used to be in "lost sheep." More than that, we are not so sure as we used to be of what a lost sheep actually *is*. We are willing to admit that we aren't so cocksure anymore of what God approves and disapproves.

We turn from the simpering piety represented by the theology of those hymns to a confession such as Malcolm Boyd's with refreshed thankfulness: "My prayer life, as the state of my spirituality, is neither very respectable nor quite correct. Needless to say, I am a self-centered man, sinfully immersed in my own welfare and concerns, attempting to manipulate God and often lost in my own self-love and self-pity." [1]

This sort of public confession on the part of Christian leaders concerning one's own inner state has become healthily prevalent. High time. We need reminding constantly that the love of God is never earned but always freely given, and that the sin above all other sins is the complacency and cold cruelty of the prayer: "God, I thank thee that I am not like other men."

But, having looked honestly and without excuse at my dried-up prayer life, my self-love and self-pity, and having admitted my complacency to my brothers, I must go on to say that I don't want to *stay* there! I don't want to remain a person "sinfully immersed in my own welfare and concerns." I want to be changed. I want to be free, not only of the guilt of my sins, but of the sins

[1] *Are You Running with Me, Jesus?* (New York: Holt, Rinehart, and Winston, 1965), p. 15.

12

themselves. If Christ can only help me see myself as I am and forgive me, but cannot *change* me, then I seriously doubt if he is a Savior at all.

I don't want to be just born again. I want to go on and grow. Having stood at the foot of the cross, and having been loved and forgiven, I want to become the creature God intended me to be. I don't want Jesus just to "run with me." I want him to run *in* me, changing the direction of my run, my power to run, and my speed. What is more, I not only want these things, but I believe that Christ has promised to do all these things.

Recently I read a horrifying description of the death by fire of a group of Albigensian Christians in the thirteenth century: "They sang hymns and cried 'Jesus,' and the devil mocked them. A fire of ordinary dry wood is much stronger than Jesus." [2]

There are many things in our lives which sometimes seem to us to be "stronger than Jesus." A college student trapped by heroin addiction, a middle-aged man gripped by a sexual affair, a housewife enslaved by alcohol or obesity; all these know that they are mastered by something which seems far stronger than Jesus. Every one of us who has been caught at some time by panic fear of failure, fear of illness, resentments, corroding memories, knows there are times when Christ still "lies in the bonds of death" as far as we are concerned.

[2] Zoe Oldenbourg, *Cities of the Flesh* (New York: Ballantine Books, 1963), p. 411.

13

It is not enough to be told at these times of real enslavement: "Christ accepts you as a faulty human being. Love and accept yourself." That is, of course, the vital first step. We can't do without that assurance. It is the meaning of Good Friday. But it is *only* the first step. Many of us wonder: Where do I go from here? What happens next? Can he release me, change me as well as love me?

And he came to Nazareth, where he had been brought up; and he went to the synagogue, as his custom was, on the sabbath day. And he stood up to read. . . . He opened the book and found the place where it was written, "The Spirit of the Lord is upon me, because he has anointed me to preach good news to the poor. He has sent me to proclaim release to the captives and recovering of sight to the blind, to set at liberty those who are oppressed."

(Luke 4:16-18)

This living Jesus Christ not only sees me as I am in loving forgiveness, but he also releases me from that which makes me unfree. He changes me. In him, we are not only reborn—we grow!

It is not enough to be made clean through Good Friday. We are to grow in power through Pentecost!

It was not enough for the prodigal son in Jesus' parable to leave the pigs. The pigs have not yet left him! Safe now in his father's house, he still has bad habits to master and new attitudes to cultivate.

The disciples sitting expectantly in the upper room

14

after Jesus had gone from their sight to the Father, knew they did not yet have what it took to change the world. They knew Jesus loved them, but they needed to grow in his power to heal the sick, raise the dead, cast out the demonic, and reconcile the hostile.

"Beloved," it was written many years later to the churches, "we are God's children now [security and acceptance]; it does not yet appear what we shall be, but we know that when he appears we shall be like him [expectancy and growth]." (I John 3:2.)

I joined an amateur choir several years ago. Once during rehearsal, the annoyed conductor told us to stop singing. "You're cheeping along like frightened orphans. Stop being apologetic. Open your mouths and sing." So we sang. Our mistakes were frightful, but he knew he couldn't get anywhere with us until we gave him our voices, mistakes and all. So we sang with the boldness of his acceptance. And as time went on, we sang with another boldness. We sang with the boldness of those who were actually learning how to sing.

The Christian makes two bold assertions: Christ loves me as I am. But Christ also changes me. The second without the first is strained insecurity. The first without the second is static and uncreative.

I am writing this book because there is hunger in the churches to hear more about the radical, exciting adventures which happen to the individual in the hands of Christ. We want to know what prayer can really do. We want to know about guidance. We want to know how to understand and discern the strange hidden

15

forces around and within us. We want to know how to break the bondage of our faults and just how to become a "new creation."

We are restless. We are no longer content with a Christianity which allows anything in the world to become for us "stronger than Jesus." Is this a selfish preoccupation in a world with starving children, napalm bombs, racial bitterness, filthy poverty, polluted water and air? Have we the right to waste one word or thought on personal growth? Is it a pathetic irrelevance in a world where millions struggle to keep alive on *any* level? I had to face this question before I dared write this book. But as I look on the lives around me and see the witness through the centuries, the answer comes repeatedly: *A person changes the world around him most radically and lastingly when he himself is radically changing and growing.*

In the midst of our work—our organizing, our teaching, our involvement—we can learn the power, the genuine power, of hourly surrender to the living Christ. Our change is not brought about by tense tinkering at ourselves. It is brought about by the radiant, immeasurable energy of Christ which has never left the world since he first said "yes" to God with no reservations. Christians do not claim to be the only lovers of God, but they do claim to be standing within a specific and unique energy field which is the person and the power of the risen Christ. Whether we express it as the life of the vine flowing into the branch, the electricity flowing through the wire, or the supreme consciousness of the

16

Person flowing into our fragmented awareness, we claim it as the energy by which we love and pray in a special way.

There is nothing so tragically ineffectual as trying to live the Christian life without the Christian power.

Try turning the other cheek without using the spiritual weapons of Christ's power to love, and see the destructive situation that develops!

Try going the second mile with the neighbor without going all the way in surrender to Christ, and see the damage done to the neighbor's personality and your own!

Try to love and pray unceasingly without turning daily to the living water of Christ, and see how quickly the personal wells run dry!

Try to use mere willpower when in the mind-obliterating grip of desire or anger, and see what it is like to try to dam up a flood with matchsticks!

Jesus Christ has not only shown us the righteous life. Many great and good men did that before his time. He has given us the power to live that righteous life. He not only shows us the beauty of God. Many great mystics had done that before his time. He gives us the means by which we can become part of that beauty. Therefore, all I say in this book about growth I say within the specific and unique vitality which is Jesus Christ still alive in the world.

Is this a *passive* theology? Does it suck the virility and challenge out of us to lay such stress on the energy of Christ? Does it turn us into children instead of mature

17

and independent adults? Many fear that this will be the result when we cease to lay stress on willpower and good intentions.

But the men and women I have observed who are the most vital, free, active, and most fearlessly themselves, are usually those who say with the Apostle Paul: "It is no longer I who live, but Christ who lives in me" (Gal. 2:20).

The living Christ, when he takes over, does not make us unfree children. We become more free. He does not thrust down the tides of life within us. He welcomes our powers and our hungers, unites them to himself, and brings them to deeper levels of powerful beauty than we had thought possible.

We want our new, active boldness in the churches to last. We want it to be deeply and permanently effective, and not to evaporate as a theological fashion. We want to continue challenging and experimenting. We want to find new and better ways of loving our brothers and fighting injustice. But I very much fear that our new eagerness will neither last nor be noticeably influential on human history if the bold humility of radical inner growth does not develop apace.

As we consider together the problems and powers of Christian growing, let us remember that it is only the living yeast which transforms the dough. The more fully we are possessed and brought to life by the living Christ, the more fully can he possess and heal the world and its suffering children.

THE CHANGE BEGINS— WHAT LIES AHEAD?

Each of us will be "handmade" by Christ. There is no assembly line in his love. Each of us is writing a unique book of Acts as he works on us and through us.

Nevertheless, there are certain basic phenomena, certain patterns of development, that one always observes in the men and women given to Christ. Four points stand out clearly and surprisingly:

(1) Christ claims the whole, not a fragmented, self.
(2) Sacrifice is a joyous paradox.
(3) The more we belong to Christ, the more we become our true selves.
(4) Our growing is not a uniform, upward progress, but a circuitous mystery.

These four basic developments are all closely related, but it is helpful to consider them separately. They are so important, and yet they are so easily misunderstood.

Take the first point, for example. What does it mean to give the whole self to Christ? Does it mean we must be a perfectly integrated person before we can belong to Christ and be used by him? Too many people interpret it that way. They have heard the warnings from the Scriptures about the importance of the single eye, serving one master, the danger of offering love to God and resentment to the neighbor, the constant threat of hypocrisy. An honest humility keeps many men and women away from Christ, because they know they cannot offer him a perfect heart. "Lord, I am not worthy to have you come under my roof" (Matt. 8: 8). "Depart from me, for I am a sinful man, O Lord" (Luke 5:8). We still tend to turn away in our proud shame.

"I didn't take Communion yesterday in church," a friend told me. "I was full of unloving thoughts and thought I'd better wait." She tried to be sincere and reverent by holding back. But the sad thing was that she had not grown to the realization that communion with Christ has the power to change her unlovely self. In effect, she was saying, "I was too sick yesterday to go to the doctor."

Sometimes I feel that the words of invitation to Communion are misleading. "You who do truly and earnestly repent of your sins, and are in love and charity

20

with your neighbors, and intend to lead a new life, . . . draw near. . . ." What if one is *not* in love and charity at the moment? What if we know our good intentions for a new life are not strong enough to make much difference? Are we to stand apart until we have accumulated the righteousness and power we lack?

A better invitation, a better prayer of wholeness, is found in Thomas à Kempis' *Imitation of Christ:*

> O Lord, I draw near as one sick to the healer, as one hungry and thirsty to the fountain of life, needy to the Kingdom of Heaven, a servant unto my Lord, a creature to my Creator, a desolate soul to my merciful comforter. . . . Behold, thou comest unto me; it is thy will to be with me; thou invitest me to thy banquet.

When caught by selfishness, jealousy, anger, self-pity, we need never refrain from prayer just because our emotions are in an unlovely condition. We need never wait until we feel more loving and religious. Swiftly we learn, not the humility that says, "Lord, I am not worthy that you should come under my roof," but rather the humility that says, "Lord, I am not worthy, so come under my roof *as fast as you can.*" We learn the wholeness of turning to him with egg all over our faces. We learn, as Agnes Sanford has gloriously said, to "sit down on the bottom rung of the ladder of sanctity and yell for Jesus Christ."

21

In fact, until we have begun to do this, we will not make any progress at all.

We learn to surrender our constructive aspects, too. This is much harder, for it is a subtler kind of relinquishment. It is fairly easy to deliver to Christ the things we are ashamed of. It is fantastically difficult to surrender to him for him to change the things we are proud of.

"I'll let Christ deal with my laziness and selfishness," we may decide. "But I can manage quite well my love for my children—that is going just fine!" But as we grow, we learn that often it is our very strong points that are standing in the way of our complete remaking. And as C. S. Lewis has wisely pointed out, it is the strong angel in each of us that can become the worst devil when out of Christ's control. Our love can become possessive. Our talent for organization can become dictatorial. Our free spontaneity can become undisciplined sloppiness.

I am not suggesting an anxious microscopic examination of ourselves. The power of Christ does not increase anxiety, it lifts it. Rather, I am suggesting that we swiftly submit all our own energies to his energy, whether they seem to need it or not. "Father, I commit to your hands and your guidance my love for my son. Use this power in me according to your will. I turn over to you these plans I am working on. Change me, wherever necessary, wherever I am blocking you and my own growth."

We learn to give him the ambiguous things. There

22

are many different sides to each of us, and often we are puzzled by ourselves. There is an emotional side. There is the cool intellectual side. There is the part that wants to be with others and there is the part that wants to be alone. What are we really? Which qualities should have priority? Which should be discouraged? We cannot always decide, but we can always turn these aspects of ourselves over to him for integration and development.

This brings us to the misunderstood matter of sacrifice. I have often felt that this is one of the most misinterpreted Christian teachings. Obviously, sacrifice is a basic need. But—sacrifice of what? We hear quoted so often the words of Jesus, "He who loses his life for my sake, will find it." But what does this mean, exactly, in our daily lives?

I have known some people who virtuously "gave up" the very things that God was trying to develop in them. What about the tired, middle-aged woman who finds herself longing for dancing classes and a new hairdo? Is that a frivolous desire she should sacrifice for Christ? Or is that longing the beginning of the birth of a new vitality and joy that is God's own gift? Perhaps a young man, as he awakens to the love of Christ, may feel he ought to give up his love for acting and go into the ministry. But perhaps God sees in him an excellent actor, and a very poor preacher.

How about ourselves? Are we called by Christ to sacrifice our occasional need to be alone when the community asks us to run a charity drive? Are we to sacrifice a strong conviction about politics or racial justice because we don't want to hurt anyone's feelings? Are we asked by Christ always to consider our own feelings and needs last?

We shall consider these questions more deeply in the chapters on guidance. At this point, I want to stress the fact that Christ does not ask us to make out the blueprint, or to be the architect of our own personalities. We can't always be sure which aspects of our growing selves should be given up or cut out. It is Christ who is making of us a new creation, not we ourselves. What a mess we make when we try!

The only kind of sacrifice that is safe, or means anything in the long run, is the joyful offering up of the whole puzzling self to Christ.As we change under his guidance, we will realize that any sacrifice entailed is not because pain is so good for us but because he wishes to prepare us for a deeper joy. For example, Christians "sacrifice" adultery not because sex is wicked, but because true commitment to our life partner teaches us far more about love. We give up an occasional, natural yen for the sake of a profounder love and joy, just as we give up talking during a concert in order to enter more fully into the musical experience.

As we grow, certain things will indeed start to break away. Some things will get crowded out. Other things that seemed natural to us will become irrelevant, insignificant, or uncomfortable. It is the living Christ who by his presence and vitality within us crowds out the things that are not right for us, not necessary for us.

24

We can trust him to do this. And we will come to realize that it is always for the sake of greater beauty and more meaningful living.

In this joyful, yet painful cleansing and plumbing of new depths, we learn that God through Christ cherishes the unique individuality of each of us. Many people are afraid that he doesn't.

"I don't want to be 'holy,' " a young man once told me. "I want to be *me!*" He had in his mind a stereotype of a typical "holy" man or woman, and quite rightly he could not see himself in that image. Does God in some way absorb us? Force us into a mold? Wash down the drain those qualities in us that make us different from all others? This fear is a real stumbling block to many persons.

But exactly the opposite happens. God does not digest us. He marries us. As love grows stronger, so do individual distinctions. Outlines become clearer. Colors stand out more brightly. Each separate leaf seems to rejoice in its "leafhood." Men and women exult in their sexual differences. The activist and the contemplative live their different lives with more vigor and less apology.

We will grow closer to each other. We will learn from each other. *But as we change and grow, we are being released to be ourselves and nobody else in all creation!* Too often we damage others by trying to make them over in our own image. Unhappy families have made this basic mistake. But the essence of Christian ecstasy and light is that each person is different and

25

precious, as is each snowflake; and the light of Christ shines through each personality like the sun shining through the contrasting radiant colors of a stained-glass window.

When "the lion lies down with the lamb," Chesterton tells us, "the lion won't become *like* a lamb." That would be "simply the lamb absorbing the lion instead of the lion eating the lamb. . . . It [Christianity] has always had a healthy hatred of pink. . . . It hates that evolution of black into white which is tantamount to a dirty gray." [1]

The genuinely "holy" people I have known are quite different from one another in appearance, politics, personality, and interests. One delights in bridge games, another in solitary canoe trips. One is an organizer, another a listener.

There are certain likenesses among these people, of course. They all look very young. It is not the youthfulness of the inexperienced and sheltered that we notice, but a kind of freshness and expectancy. They are never bored. Neither are they boring. It is always a delight to talk with them because their sense of humor is keen, and there is a deep sensitivity to beauty and pain. Oddly enough, they are less dependent on beauty and less crushed by pain than are the rest of us. It is helpful to talk with them, for they don't judge or categorize us. At the same time, they see right through

[1] G. K. Chesterton, *Orthodoxy* (London: John Lane Company, 1908), pp. 179 and 181.

our masks. They involve themselves in our troubles, but they honor our freedom. Most of them didn't begin with these qualities. Much less did they set out to manufacture them. Rather, the lovable Christ shines through their lovableness.

A next great surprise is the discovery that our growing is a mystery of starts and stops. Sometimes we seem to shoot upward, breathlessly, into new insights and powers. Then all of a sudden we find we are apparently motionless on a plateau. For a while we may find ourselves even sliding downhill. Then, there we are on a mountain peak, seeing an undreamed view, completely uncertain how we got there.

Later we shall look more deeply into the various reasons for our staggering, zigzag progress. And as we look back down the path in our growing maturity, we will understand better why at this point we moved so swiftly, and why at that stage we stood still in darkness. But the Christian should be warned at the very beginning of his commitment that his growth will not always be smooth or easily understood. The hands of Christ are guiding us not only through the obvious obstacles but also through our subconscious resistances.

Also, Christ will not let us rest long at any one stage of development. We may think we have arrived. We may think we have found the method of prayer, service, self-expression that will forever be a source of energy for us. But he will always surprise us by breaking the old idols and urging us past the comfortable resting place.

27

After a person has crossed a certain plane, . . . he comes up against a wall. To enter the new segment of his way he must jump this wall or be carried over it. . . . The earnest Christian constantly comes up against a boundary, finds he has reached the limits of his previous religious experience and cannot continue straight on. His customary forms of faith, hope, and love and prayer simply cease to serve, and he must seek new ways by which new depths of his soul may open up, be plumbed and taken possession of.[2]

This is a necessary insight for all growing Christians, whether young, middle-aged, or elderly. Perhaps those in the middle years need this challenge most, for those are the years of even greater restlessness, frustration, and potentiality than the highly publicized years of adolescence. There is a reason for the deep hungers and questionings of the late thirties and mid-forties. It is the time when deep-lying energies, yet untapped, rise to the surface to be used. Now that the great choices of marriage, profession, and children have been made and the outer structure of life has been settled, it is the time for the challenge of the profound spiritual energies. The swiftest growing, the most lasting changes can now begin.

Unfortunately many middle-aged men and women misinterpret this restlessness and desire for change as a signal for a new job, a new mate, or a new country.

[2] Ida Gorres, *The Hidden Face* (London: Burns & Oats, 1959), p. 106.

Except in a few instances, these outer changes will not long satisfy the deep longing. It is the call from God's spirit in each of us to keep growing in new ways. There is nothing wrong with our questioning and rebellion. There would be something seriously wrong with us if we never felt it! But we should know it for what it is, the urge from our deepest selves never to "settle down." The outer frameworks of our lives are not fences to keep us from change. They are just the raw material with which to start the real adventures. It is not an accident that almost without exception the greatest saints, prophets, and reformers have been men and women who received their deep calling and commission in their thirties or forties.

The big adventures can begin for each of us today. In the living hand of the living Christ, there are no limits to the possibilities. Each day, as we deliver ourselves again into those gentle, but firm hands, we can pray with eagerness, "Christ, make me new again today."

29

FRONTIERS OF PRAYER

I heard it again the other day—that same old tired approach to prayer. "Prayer inspires us to greater activity," said the speaker. "Prayer is a retreat from activity for a while, which leads to greater activity and love."

It is exactly this emphasis that makes prayer seem so boring and futile to many Christians. Obviously it has a lot of truth in it. Everyone admits we ought to let ourselves be more inspired through a prayer discipline. We admit it with yawns and a bit of guilty resentment. It is similar to being told we ought to go on a diet, or answer our letters regularly, or do morning exercises, all for our own good.

Most of us by now have tried out a few daily prayer

disciplines, just as we have tried morning exercises. And likewise most of us have drifted away from it, thankful to be released from such an exhausting, irrelevant routine. In the future, we decide, we will just get our inspiration in more pleasant ways, through music, for example, or nature or art or talking with our friends.

A young minister confided to us recently: "I admit that the discipline of prayer is probably a very fine thing. But I also admit that I seem to be getting along without it quite well!"

Sometimes we go a step further and redefine prayer as anything which brings us in closer touch with the world around us. We explain to ourselves and others that in these days of split-second timing, instant decisions, constant noise, and unending demands on our time and energy, we must find modern ways of praying suitable for our culture. Therefore, we reason, any act of love, any deep involvement with others, any participation in art or beauty, anything that makes us more human is prayer in the deepest sense.

But underneath this earnest reasoning there lies in most of us a wistfulness, a hunger, a feeling of missing out on something that just might change life with undreamed depth of power and beauty.

This latent, hungry hope arises from a true instinct. We are quite right to rebel from prayer as it is usually presented to us. It was never meant to be boring. It was never meant to be mere inspiration to bigger and better action. It was never intended as an exhausting spiritual gymnastic, leading (perhaps) to mystical ex-

31

perience. *Prayer does not merely lead us to power. Prayer is itself power.* And prayer becomes alive to us perhaps for the first time when we have finally realized this.

When we are in the hands of Christ being changed and turn to the Father in prayer, at that moment we are enveloped by a power and presence far greater than our own. If we could see at that moment what is actually going on, we would see that the light encompassing us is brighter and more brilliant than the sun, and is bringing about greater, more radical changes.

This is not poetry. It is sober fact. Someday our scientists, as well as our theologians, will know a great deal more than any of us do now about the mysterious forces moving through us which are channeled by prayer. But we can begin now to make our own discovery that when we pray a weapon whose magnitude we cannot measure is put into our hands.

Alexis Carrell, scientist and physician, once wrote: "Prayer is the most important form of energy that one can generate. In prayer we link ourselves with the inexhaustible power that spins the universe."

Those who approach prayer as energy released almost never drop it later in fatigue, disillusionment, or boredom. When we realize that this power is an objective fact, a law of the universe, we realize that it has nothing to do with our fluctuating emotional moods and that it makes no demands on our personal charisma. It exists whether we choose to do anything about it or not. All we need is a willingness to be part of it.

32

"When we abide in Christ, our tiny will becomes an atom in his almighty will, and in his name we speak spiritual continents into being."[1]

The burden of subjectivity, the strain of turning ourselves into a source of power and discipline, is lifted from us. All that is required of us is to put ourselves into this energy field by saying: "Lord, pray in me and through me. Make me your channel." He will do the rest.

As we learn to pray in this objectivity we will also see increasing evidence that Jesus Christ is very much alive and active in this world. The book of Acts has never been closed. We are still writing chapters in it. The age of miracles has just begun.

"Prayer is not a gentle pastime," observes the new Dutch Roman Catholic catechism. Too many of our church leaders think of it as a gentle, placid occupation like tea-brewing and ceramics. Something suitable for gentle old ladies. But as we grow in the power of prayer we will rapidly change our minds about both prayer *and* the old ladies!

The exciting realization grows that we are not begging a reluctant God to do something, nor are we informing an ignorant God about something. We begin to discover that it is *we,* not God, who have been reluctant and ignorant. All along God has wanted to do much more for us and through us than we have wanted him to do.

[1] Helen Shoemaker, *Secret of Effective Prayer* (New York: Fleming H. Revell Co., 1967), p. 31.

33

"You are loved ultimately. You are loved creatively. You are loved endlessly." This is the way our minister recently described the Father's relationship with us. If indeed we are loved that way, then prayer is certainly no pleading with a cold, elusive God. It is making contact with a God of fire who seeks to enflame our own cold, elusive lives. His is the endless light that beats on the closed doors and windows of our dark, shut wills.

When we pray for the peace of the world, we are not begging God for anything. He wants peace much more than we do. Rather, we are giving ourselves at that moment of prayer to the divine energy, permitting it to work through us. His is the power. We are the surrendered channels.

When we pray for a girl who is a drug addict, we are not begging God to do the right thing by that girl. He already knows all about her and loves her much more than we do. Instead when we pray we are surrendering our wills to him. By holding her in his healing light God works through us to help bring about a creative change in her.

At the very moment of surrendered prayer, an immeasurable power is being released into the situation, into the world. *Something always happens when we pray through Christ.*

In this exciting approach to prayer, all the usual categories—adoration, confession, petition—become filled with new and powerful meaning. We will not always feel the power and the drama, because our feelings rise and fall like the tides. But as we grow we will

34

enter into a knowing, a confidence of power, that cuts far deeper than feelings.

Take the prayer of adoration, for example. Seldom do we actually have an intense awareness of the presence of God. Trying to whip up such an awareness, straining after it, exhausts us more quickly than anything else. But when we are held by the power of the living Christ, we know that even if we can't feel or see the Father, Christ can. He lifts our feeble gropings straight to the heart of God himself. In Christ's own perfect vision of the Father, he will do the work in our souls that is done only through adoration. We can relax and trust ourselves to God. He will lead us along the path of awareness as swiftly as we are able to follow it.

I am all in favor of the new efforts in our churches to bring about new depths of adoration through developing the sensory awareness of the sacraments of color, taste, hearing, and touch. It is no longer a strange thing these days to enter a church or seminary and see some sarape-clad young person in the pulpit with his guitar, or to see a young congregation feeding each other cookies for Communion, dancing under the trees while singing a hymn. These are new and hopeful ways that seek ardently to respond to the eternal call of God to the awakening soul in each of us, "Arise my love, and come . . ."

But even these appealingly lovely new ways of worship can become pathetic gimmicks or exhausting and rigid forms if undertaken in the conviction that the power of adoration is a subjective thing, depending solely on our human efforts. Any new means of worship is good if it is a dancing and an adoring based on the fact of God and not on our feeling about him.

Many young people who have been taught that adoring is the same as feeling seek to force the pace through drugs or occult ascetic disciplines. Something undoubtedly will be experienced. But even if it is a beautiful experience, far too often the person is not ready for it and does not know what to do with it or how to make it part of his daily life. Christ is not out to give us new thrills. He is out to make of each of us a new creation.

Nevertheless, as we slowly grow in Christ, hints are given to us daily of what adoration will be when finally we shall see fully and we "will know, even as we have been known."

"What will heaven really be like?" asked my daughter. I thought it over and said, "Heaven will be a lot like the way you feel on Christmas Eve when all the candles are lit." She got it at once. She realized that heaven, or the fullness of adoration, is not a static state. It is a combination of unity and vitality. It is a state in which endless potentialities are unfolding, and also in which one's hungry need is fully fed.

Choose your own moment as a hint of what full adoration—full heaven—will be. Think of an experience when you were all energy, yet all peace; when you were both eager and awed. Think of a moment which fed you utterly with its meaning, and yet challenged you to explore even further. It might be the moment

36

when you first saw the mountains or the sea. It might be the hour of deep communication with a friend. It might be the instant of ecstasy when a difficult intellectual problem is finally grasped. Perhaps it was the moment of giving birth to a baby. Perhaps it was the time of challenge of working in a garden, or painting, or writing. Maybe it was the time you threw yourself joyfully into work for better politics or racial justice.

Whatever the moment for each of us, we learned a little more about God, not only as lawgiver, but also as everlasting beauty. We learned something about the "fullness of joy" for which he made us. This is a hint of what adoration can be, and as we grow, increasingly will be. God will forever feed us with his beauty and joy as we increase our capacity to receive more of him. This is nothing to be strained after. We cannot force this feeling and this growth. It is a gift that will increasingly be received. We can pray our prayer of adoration in this expectation, with gratitude for the hints already received.

Confession comes alive for us as our adoration grows. As we become more aware of the beauty of God, we also become more sorrowfully aware of our resistance to it. There is something in each of us which pulls back from growing experience in fear or fatigue. There is something perverse in each of us which says: "I won't grow bigger than I am now. It might hurt. It might ask more of me than I want to give."

We become uncomfortably aware that our motives are always mixed. It is a shock, but also a step forward, when we face the fact, for example, that we deeply resent someone whom we also love. It is usually not a gentle thing—the sight of our own heart. But God gives us as we grow a new, stern strength to face it. In the wisdom of his love, we are often shielded in the early days of our commitment. We are not always shown the full sight of our heart in the beginning. God takes us as fast as we are able to go.

But it is equally disconcerting—perhaps more so—when we are able to look fully at the positive aspects of ourselves. It is a sign of genuine growth when in the confession of prayer we look at something in us that is good and are able to praise God delightedly and objectively. As we grow in dependence on him, our masks of false pride drop away. We learn that all good, loving, creative impulses are his gift, and we can be as happy about them when they are found in ourselves as when found in anyone else.

"You have certainly become a warm, spontaneous person," a friend may tell us. And in the objective honesty which grows in us we are free now to take a quick look at ourselves and think joyfully: "Yes, I am changing in that way. I thank the Lord of life who makes it possible."

There is another important thing we learn as we grow in our prayer of confession and honesty. A wise friend once told me: "God does not stop at our skin." The darkroom image I have so often used, with us shut up in our dark withdrawal inside and the light of God beating on the outside, is a useful image up to a point.

38

But like all images, it has serious limitations. It is apt to give us a feeling of apartness from God as though he were only outside our darkness. This is not true. God not only challenges and calls us with his light, but he also joins us in our darkness and limitations. In our anguish, doubt, fear, and ignorance he is right there holding us. Otherwise we would have no way of knowing that it was dark or that light was available.

Our faults, our guilts, should not make us feel that we are in any way separated from him. Even if there is some sin we feel we cannot yet relinquish to him, still we are with him. Several people have told me they were often keenly aware of God's love surrounding them, even though they were also fully aware they were disobeying him. This is a most necessary thing to learn as we grow in prayer, because very often we will fail in our prayer disciplines, and many days may go by when we do not pray. If we permit a sense of guilt, at that point, to drive a wedge between us and God, then we will feel increasingly uncomfortable at the very thought of prayer. The very thing that was designed to lift the burdens off us will itself become an added burden of guilt and resentment. This need not be. We can keep growing even in the grip of weakness or guilt by confessing our helplessness to him with honest simplicity. We can grow by learning anew that we need him every minute, most of all in the minutes of guilt and lethargy.

We are taught in our Christian faith that the structures of evil and darkness have no power of their own.

39

Ultimately all energy, all power, comes from God. Evil, Satan, darkness—call it what you will—draws on the power of the Father and then distorts it. It cannot create; it can only twist. "You would have no power over me at all," said Jesus to Pilate, "unless it was given to you from above." So whether we are in the grip of our own evil or someone else's, God is right there with us. Perhaps his suffering is even greater than ours in that it is his own energy, his own creation, which is being twisted and distorted.

But the agencies of darkness that misuse God's own energy will not have the last word. In the Old Testament we are promised: "They shall not hurt or destroy in all my holy mountain; for the earth shall be full of the knowledge of the Lord as the waters cover the sea" (Isa. 11:9). In the New Testament we are told: "The creation waits with eager longing for the revealing of the sons of God; . . . the creation itself will be set free from its bondage to decay and obtain the glorious liberty of the children of God" (Rom. 8:19-21).

As we grow through prayer in the understanding of ourselves, we become aware of two great things: God is with us, even in our darkness. But God's own deepest energy is even now breaking the power of that darkness.

NEW DEPTHS OF INTERCESSION

"The creation itself will be set free from its bondage to decay." This confidence, underlying our prayer of confession, is the same trust that enables us to ask God for anything. Actually, as we grow, we learn that intercession is not really asking at all. It is cooperating with the God whose will it is to set this creation free from its decay.

We will not grow much in the expectancy of intercession—prayer for others—until we realize that the Father of Jesus Christ is not a God who sends illness and tragedy. He does not educate, punish, or test us by the deliberate infliction of suffering.

It used to be a frequent ministerial consolation to

write to some bereaved or stricken person: "My dear friend, I have heard the hand of God rests heavily upon you." Parents would fear that a child had died because they loved him too much and thus had "tempted God." People believed that a little town would be wiped out through a plague because its inhabitants had sinned in some way. A paralyzed young woman would resign herself to a life spent in bed "because it pleases God to keep me here."

Or it might be taught, as in the song of "The Blind Ploughman," that God is the kind of God who might "take away my eyes, that my soul might see."

Probably this belief has enabled many good people to endure perplexing illness or tragedy with courage. An arthritic patient recently said wearily to me: "I wish I *did* believe that God was sending me all this pain. It would be so much easier if I felt there was a purpose in it." But this is not the God we see through Jesus Christ. Jesus always spoke of illness as a demonic force which he healed whenever he could. Can we seriously imagine Jesus saying to a blind man: "My friend, accept your blindness as God's will. He caused it so your soul might see"! One hopes that during the years of blindness the man did indeed use the time of waiting by becoming more spiritually sensitive and loving. I know three or four blind people who are deeply advanced in spiritual growth. Their time has not been wasted. With the help of God, they have used the evil thing that came upon them and wrested good from it. But this is not at all the same thing as believing that God sent the blind-

42

ness, or that he wants it as an educational tool, or that such things will have a place in his ultimate kingdom. Nature is not God. Nature is only part of his creation. Nature can make mistakes, develop along blind alleys, and sometimes give space to evil. As we are told in the Epistle to the Romans, all nature groans and travails, even as we do.

Of all the evils that God the loving Father has endured from us through all these centuries, I am convinced the very worst is our stubborn conviction that he has sent the agonies that beset us. So many people are afraid of him. So many people think he is jealous and disapproving of joy, abundance, and health. Even those who have intellectually thrown over that concept of God are still often subconsciously haunted by the image of a disapproving old man spying on them from the sky.

The cross? Of course there is the cross. And all Christians are pledged to share it. But the cross is not illness or accident. The cross is the sacrificial burden we choose freely to carry for another in the spirit of love. This is the suffering that Christ invites us to share. It is the kind of suffering that truly deepens us and leads us into profound sharing of the nature of God himself. The cross is the surrendering of our ego demands, our very life if necessary for the sake of justice, lovingkindness, and reform. This has nothing to do with the evils of illness or accident.

So when we pray for others, we are neither begging God nor wrestling with him. We begin to grow to new depths of intercession as we realize that our loving

43

concern for our friend is just a faint shadow of what God already feels. We can relax. He already wants to bring about a healing in the situation, and he wants to use us as channels.

This poses real difficulty for some people. Why are intermediaries needed at all? Why can't God in his infinite power bring about a healed relationship or a healed body directly? A friend once said to me sadly: "I must conclude that God either *can't* heal me or *won't* heal me. And I don't know which is worse."

But there is a third alternative. God wants to bring about healing. He is certainly able to do anything in his creation. But out of his love, out of his gift of freedom to us all, he chooses to work his loving, healing will through channels, mediums. In this way we his creatures are taught how to love, how to share burdens, how to share his creativity. By working through us to help someone else, God also helps us! Water, flowing through a channel, certainly wets the channel as well as the field beyond.

When my eleven-year-old prays for her little newly planted tree, she is not only working with God lovingly on the tree; God at that moment is working also on her. As we pray for each other, God's fire and power burns in us both.

Apparently, for the full healing will of God to become operative in any situation, there must be on the part of someone a full, free awareness, consent, and trust. This is the reason for the Roman Catholic's veneration of Mary. She surrendered body and will to God's Spirit and made it possible for the Christ to become flesh at that point of history. In a smaller way, we are doing the same thing every time we turn ourselves over to God as a channel of help for someone else.

Some people find it helpful to visualize some symbol of their mediumship. Perhaps you can picture yourself as a branch firmly connected to the strong trunk of a tree. Or perhaps you can hold pictures in mind as a television antenna catches the invisible vibrations in the air to bring pictures to the set. These are helpful symbols of what we are when we pray for another person. The power passes through us. Then we can hold in mind the person for whom we are praying. Perhaps we can picture him also as a branch of that tree. Or, as a friend suggested to me once, we can picture him stepping into a room filled with light. Or we can see him held in God's hand, or imagine him with Christ laying his hands upon him.

These are only suggestions. It is not really necessary to picture anything at all. It is quite sufficient to ask the living, healing Jesus Christ to do any necessary picturing for us and take it from there. There are no rigid rules about this at all. Whatever we picture, whatever method we find helpful, it is only necessary to remember that the healing streams come from God, not from us. I have seen great psychic and physical exhaustion result when a person tried to be the source, rather than the channel of healing.

When we put God through Christ first in our prayer for another, we won't make the mistake of concentrating on the particular illness or problem. When we pray about Mr. Smith's perforated ulcer and the shaky marriage of Mr. and Mrs. Brown, we will find that our mind is no longer concentrating anxiously on the ulcer and the unhappy marriage, but rather on the all-enveloping love and power of the Father. As the old hymn reads: "The thought of Thee is mightier far than sin and pain and sorrow are." This is the secret of powerful prayer for others.

God gives us people to pray for. Sometimes we see a face which remains in our minds for weeks, or even years. We don't know why, but it stays with us. I look on it as a definite call to prayer for that person for as long as the memory of him returns to us. Or perhaps we read some news item that compels us to deep concern, and we find the persons involved repeatedly coming to mind. Or we suddenly find ourselves thinking vividly of some friend for no apparent reason. It may be someone we know well, or it may be someone we have not seen or thought about much for years.

A few years ago I began to think of an old friend I had not heard from in a long time. I could not imagine any reason why he kept coming so persistently to mind. Finally I wondered if it was a signal to pray for him, and I began to do so. A few months later he came to town unexpectedly and contacted me. During the evening's conversation he told me that he had just recently found his faith again after years of agnosticism and had joined a church. He had begun to rethink his attitude to

46

faith around the time I began to receive the signals for prayer.

Another example of this happened a few weeks ago. One of my prayer group members asked me one Sunday morning what I had been doing the previous afternoon. "About two o'clock," she said, "I suddenly began to think of you very intensely. So I turned off my radio and held you in God's light for a while. Is everything all right?" It had been at exactly 2:00 P.M. the day before that three college students had come to me with some serious concerns. I was using all my energies to meet their need and was at my wit's end at some points. Apparently I had sent out a signal for help without consciously realizing it and my friend was "tuned in."

If we are asking Christ to deepen us in prayer, random thoughts about other people are not always so random after all. Continually God uses us this way to help one another.

In the same way we hold in his light certain concerns, world or community, that are on our hearts, such as child abuse, racial and student riots, atmosphere and water pollution, war and poverty. Even though these are wide, general concerns, we can ask to be used as channels for their healing.

It is a good thing at some point in prayer (whether group or individual) to surrender one's self to God's use as a channel for anyone in the world who at that moment is in desperate need of prayer. For a few moments we should hold ourselves in willingness to be used for any such person or purpose. It is my faith

47

that God works through us creatively and mightily at such a time. People have told me that they are more "aware" of the presence and power moving through them in this prayer than in any other. We will probably never know in this world the results of such prayers. But it is a growing conviction with me that this is what we are to do and to do frequently. We will leave the results to him.

I have also learned that it is especially helpful to pray for someone when he is asleep. At such times the defenses and rationalizations of surface consciousness are lowered, and the deep subconscious is more open and accessible. I have found this is extremely effective with children. If a child is facing some problem, whether physically or emotionally, it is well to go into his room after he is asleep, sit quietly beside him, perhaps lay a hand lightly on him, and surround him with thoughts of the loving power of God. We relinquish him into the hands of that God who understands him and loves him far better than we ever can. But it is not necessary to be physically with the person we are praying for. If we wake in the night, for example, and can't sleep again, it is an excellent time to pray for our friends. It should be a prayer of trust and tranquillity— and it is a prayer of great power.

This is *not* thought control, hypnosis, or brainwashing! Prayer in Christ becomes the prayer of deep respect for another's free will and decision. We can't force another to say "yes" to God or to change his actions and attitudes. Any prayer which tries to batter down

48

another's door or to dominate or control is no prayer in Christ. But we can, through prayer, knock on a door and offer to share what we have found.

Oddly enough, it is much more difficult to pray for ourselves than for other people. Several people, deeply practiced in prayer, have told me that they just can't bring themselves to do it. Others say that even when they do there seem to be very scanty results.

There may be two reasons for this. One, we somehow are ashamed to pray for ourselves. We think it self-centered, and we feel that as Christians we ought to be using all our concerns for others. Two, we are apt to get tense and panicky about ourselves, as well as emotionally shortsighted.

It is part of true growing in Christ that this kind of praying (petition, as it is generally called) slowly becomes both possible and more effective. It may be one of the delayed gifts that come our way. We can help pave the way for it by remembering that Jesus Christ always treated each person's plea for his own healing with great respect. He never said or implied, "Why do you come whining to me? You ought to be thinking about others. Aren't you ashamed?" Nor did he ever say, "You wouldn't have had this problem in the first place if you had had sufficient faith!"

The first year I led a prayer group I had a low-grade infection which sapped my energy for several weeks. However, I kept doggedly turning up each week to lead the group in spite of a fever, because I was frankly ashamed to admit that I, the leader of an intercessory group, was sick enough to need to stay at home and ask for the prayers of others. I kept nervously thinking of the unconsciously comical notice that appeared in a newspaper, "The Clairvoyant Society will not meet tomorrow night, due to unforeseen circumstances"! I could just imagine some church member thinking sarcastically, "Physician, heal thyself!"

But this is just where I made my mistake. I had forgotten that *I* was not the great Physician. I was merely a branch of that great vine and sometimes, like any other branch, I would need help and pruning. I would have shown far more respect for my group and far more faith in my own doctrine if I had said simply: "I am sick. I need help tonight. I am going to rest at home, and I am asking you to meet and hold me in the healing light." This would not have been selfishness. It would have been merely good sense and a more genuine Christianity. What is more, it would have been far more helpful to others than my limping along feeling like a hypocrite. We learn, as we grow, to look at our own needs with the same objectivity and respect with which we regard our faults and our good points.

We learn slowly to relinquish to him our whole self —not just the immediate problem. We realize, as we ask for healing or guidance, that this is not a reluctant God hiding in the heavens while we desperately seek him. Much less is he a stodgy disapproving old man speaking in tremolo organ tones. He is joy itself and unutterable beauty. He is the unexpected. To grow in awareness of him is *fun*. He takes us along ways we had not dreamed of, and he wants us to wake each morning with the eager thought, "What does he plan for me today? What will he do through me today?"

We know there is no such thing as unanswered prayer. But the answers are usually unexpected and sometimes surprising. So we must keep alert and aware of answers coming to us along unorthodox channels. We can be very practical and down-to-earth about this. We can commit to God the difficult letter we have to write, and new ideas start forming. We can mentally turn over to him a quarrelsome committee and hold the separate member in His light during the meeting. Watch what happens! We can approach a counseling session not knowing what to say, or sit down to write a sermon, or a book, or a speech, and find ideas forming that we didn't even know we had. We can commit to him the antipathy we feel toward someone and find new unexpected depths of compassion opening in us. We can give him any pain, any problem, any closed door or dead end in our lives. He will take it. And something will happen.

I could continue for many pages giving examples I have seen of the quiet miracles that happen in daily life through surrendered prayer. They are swift, unpredictable, challenging, often amusing, and always to the point. Sometimes they reach a deeper point than we had in mind. God has a way of doing radical surgery not only on the particular problem we referred to him, but on several other problems as well that we had preferred to overlook at present.

51

49877   STANLEY LIBRARY
FERRUM JUNIOR COLLEGE

No, prayer is not a "gentle pastime." When we expose our whole self to God's reality, we are changing as radically as when we expose our bodies to cobalt. The deepest tissues of our lives are being irradiated and changed. Obstacles are being burned away. New life and energy are being deeply implanted. We may feel no particular emotional change for a long time. But the change will soon make itself known in many practical ways. Christ *is* practical. And he is immediate. He is with us at the turn of a thought.

Whenever I have prayed in recent months, I have held a thought given me by George Fearnehough, microbiologist and prayer leader, "Jesus told us 'I am the light of the world.' And always remember—the most remarkable thing of all about light is *the speed of its coming!*"

WHAT ABOUT GUIDANCE?

The question of guidance arouses strong party feelings. There are few concepts which evoke such nonsense at one extreme and such bullheaded resistance at the other. We all know only too well about the nonsense. We know the kind of woman who says God "guides" her each morning as she chooses which dress to wear. I knew a woman who was sure God was guiding her to marry a certain man. The fact that the man paid her no attention whatever made not the slightest difference in her conviction. And what about the two ministers who recently shepherded their congregations to another state because God "told" them their part of the country was to be destroyed by an earthquake?

Given enough of this sort of thing, many intelligent

Christians start looking glassy-eyed when guidance is mentioned. Or they start getting resentful. Or they politely keep quiet about it, but are convinced that persons claiming guidance are fooling themselves.

Is there any reality underlying the nonsense? Is the whole concept of guidance something we ought to have outgrown in the twentieth century? And if there is guidance, how can it be distinguished from illusion or rationalization?

Of course we must realize that as soon as any radiant reality is discovered, no matter what it is, there will be pathetic people who misunderstand and distort it. This happens all the time in politics, theology, and new scientific discoveries. It is the plague of all serious researchers and innovators. It is not the enemies of a new idea who endanger it. It is the foolish friends, who by their exaggerations and distortions bring scorn upon the whole thing. Anytime a Christian leader preaches on guidance he is sure to be buttonholed after the sermon and made to listen to an enthusiastic account of how the Bible verse picked at random was such a perfect message for the women next door, or how the inner "hunch" led her to just the right shop with a dress sale going on that very day! More tragically, he may observe families breaking up and churches being divided because a few individuals insisted on their own personal guidance without any reference whatever to the well-being of others.

On one occasion, after I had preached on guidance, a young woman stopped to speak to me on her way out of church. "I agreed with everything you said," she told me in obvious sincerity. "That's exactly what I believe about guidance, too." I happened to know that this young woman had recently moved in with a man separated from his wife. They were not considering marriage. Children were involved. Families on both sides were in deep distress. The young woman claimed she felt "guided" to take this step.

Amusingly enough, a man also stopped to agree with me after this same sermon. He too "agreed with everything" I had said about guidance. He had recently joined a certain religious cult with a rigid judgmental theology open to no new ideas whatever from the outside.

The fact that both these people, living by diametrically opposed standards of ethics, could hear the same sermon on guidance and each solemnly aver that he "agreed with everything" I had said made me think either it had been a very vague sermon, or else each had such a fixed idea about guidance that he didn't really hear what had been said. In either case, the families and friends of this young woman and man perhaps will always have a thoroughly disillusioned view of anything resembling "guidance." To them, it will probably be just another name for doing what you want to do anyway.

Paul Tournier, the Swiss psychiatrist, once wrote:

The assurance of the mental patient who believes himself to be endowed with divine authority is in marked contrast with the hesitant humility of healthy people, the genuineness of whose spirituality we sense at once. . . . Even apart from any question of mental disturbance, the doctor knows how an unconscious psychological complex can mislead a man of good faith on what he believes to be a command from God.[1]

However, having admitted this constant danger, I must go on to witness that there *is* a solid reality in the concept of direct guidance from God. If God is the lover of the world; if Christ yet lives, not as a myth or a memory but in fact; if he shares with us his strength and light; then the concept of guidance becomes a natural, obvious thing. There is nothing occult about it. There is nothing mystical or mysterious about it. It is the practical, down-to-earth result of the opening and sensitizing of the personality to the living God. It is part of the growing ability of the maturing soul to recognize what the living God is doing.

Let us look first at what the best criteria of genuine guidance *are not*. There are two main misinterpretations.

Strong feelings, hunches, and inner commands are not trustworthy. This can never be repeated too often. These things rise and fall like waves of the ocean. They vary according to the state of our digestions. They waver and shift according to the latest book we have read or the interesting people we have talked to. They emerge with discontented and restless times of our

[1] *The Adventure of Living* (New York: Harper & Row, 1965).

lives. They subside disconcertingly, leaving us feeling like fools. This goes for actual voices and visions, too. Some people really do have them. They may, like feelings and hunches, be part of genuine guidance, but on their own they are not trustworthy evidence.

Second (and this is more surprising), a strong conviction of duty is not a trustworthy guide. Some of us are suspicious of anything that gives us satisfaction. Some of us feel that whatever gives us genuine happiness and fulfillment cannot possibly be the will of God for us.

There is an old poem which used to be worked on samplers, hung on walls, preached at children, and quoted in sermons: "I slept and dreamed that life is beauty. I woke and found that life is duty." This is an abominable interpretation of guidance. It is just as misleading and tragic as the conviction that whatever we want is right for us. To be sure, we are often led by hard, challenging ways. But if it is God's own true guidance, there will also be growing joy, growing beauty. *There is one strong reliable sign of genuine guidance: the facts and realities which emerge after we commit our problem to God.*

When John the Baptist sent to inquire if Jesus were truly the Messiah, Jesus did not answer, "I know I am the Messiah because I have always felt I was, and besides that I have had visions and voices telling me so." Nor did he answer: "I am the Messiah because *someone* has to be, and I feel it my duty to undertake the role." No, he pointed to the facts. He said in effect,

57

"Look around. What do you see? The sick are healed. The dead are raised. The poor have good news told them." In short, look at the fruits. Look at the results. Look at the facts.

Let us look at our own lives now. The realities that surround us before we have given ourselves to God are not always the will of God for us. There are such things as facts and realities which are either evil in themselves or wrong for us. We have all known people in jobs that are not right for them. We have known marriages that should not have taken place. We all have known people in situations that do not represent the best they can be. When we are caught in a destructive situation, it is not a true understanding of God's will to say: "This is God's will for me. I will just have to bear it as a cross." In the next chapter we shall consider more fully the tests by which we can judge whether our present situation is destructive or right for us. God can and will bring new realities, new facts into our lives, after we give him our problems.

First we must look at our situation with honesty and face our feelings about it. We can't push our genuine feelings out of sight. They will only make themselves felt in another way. We must admit to ourselves that we are unhappy, bewildered, caught in some way. Then we look to the Father. It doesn't matter if we are not in a pious mood at the moment; we can look to him no matter how we feel and give the problem to him. This is not so easy. We have a way of giving him our problems and then going our way still anxiously dragging them with us. We have to hand the problem to God as simply and directly as we would hand over a parcel to a friend who wishes to carry it for us. Then we go off about our business. If the worry pops up again, and it will, since we are human, we must remind ourselves firmly, "I have given this problem to God. He is carrying it now. He is going to solve it and show me what to do."

Then we must watch in alertness and expectancy. Something is going to happen! There will come a change in the facts. It may not be at all the change expected. It may come almost immediately, or it may take a while. But we can absolutely count on it. A door will open. A chance will be offered. A new person will come into our lives, or an unexpected side of a person already known will be revealed. Or a new idea will come. There will be a definite change in the realities around us, and in the changing facts we will see the genuine guidance from God.

A young minister I know was becoming increasingly unhappy and restless in his work. Instead of resigning himself to unhappiness, he gave the problem to the Father. Within a few weeks he began to realize some facts about himself that he had not really thought through before. He realized that he had always had an excellent head for business. He loved mathematics and questions of finance. Accepting this fact about himself, he was not too surprised in a few weeks when he was offered a job as financial and investment advisor. He is extremely happy now and does much good in assisting ministers and churches in their financial tangles.

A young friend of ours was a heavy cigarette smoker. He had tried in every way to fight smoking by will-power. But as soon as he made promises to himself and his family he would break them. Finally he faced the fact that he was helpless. He could not stop alone. He handed the problem to God and wondered with alert expectancy what God would do about it. The answer came when he felt suddenly inspired to write a book he had been thinking about writing for some years. He began it at once. During the enthralled first week he forgot all about cigarettes, and from then on it was not nearly as hard to abstain. In the new enthusiasm and hard work of writing the desire to smoke eventually left him altogether.

When I first began to take a serious interest in prayer, I didn't know where to find the right person or group who could teach me. So I asked God to send me the right person. Within a few days a secretary, whom I knew slightly, phoned me. She was the last person I would have expected to be sent me. She was a person with a sparkling sense of humor, fashionably dressed, and interested in bridge and pretty hats. But it seems she was also a person of deep, rich experience in prayer, by which she had surmounted many tragic experiences. She invited me to join an ecumenical prayer group of which she was leader. I would never have thought to go to her myself with questions. But she was exactly the person I needed.

A lonely, troubled young woman confided to me that all avenues seemed closed to her. Her health seemed to be on the decline, her studies, which formerly had delighted her, were no longer satisfying. Church work didn't seem to help either. Where should she turn? What should she do? Frankly, I didn't know. I couldn't tell her what would help. So we agreed to pray about it and turn the whole matter over to the Father.

I had expected the answer to come through some deep mystical inspiration, or some engrossing charitable work, or some new, enthralling study, for she was a scholar who was deeply religious and charitable. But the answer came in a completely unexpected way, as it usually does. A friend dropped by one day and casually referred to a series of evening dance lessons being given in town. This young woman overheard, and before I knew it she had enrolled in the dance classes, bought herself some pretty new dresses, and before long had found some splendid new friends. I never saw such a change in a person in so short a time. God had known that what she needed was not more church work or studying, but some gaiety, color, and joyous dancing.

Such an example is startling to people who don't expect to find God moving through such channels. But I have always remembered a wise, pungent saying I read somewhere: *"Whatever gave us the idea that God is exclusively interested in religion?"*

God is interested in everything. Is that not natural, considering he is the source of all the burning, creative energy of the universe? He didn't merely create saints and angels. Walk through a zoo or aquarium some day

61

if you want to see the extent to which his humor and creativity go! We can afford to be literally openmouthed as well as open-eyed in our expectancy. He the living is also the startling!

And as we wait for answers to our problems, for guidance, we will remember that he will come to us in a way we do not expect. A new fact will come into our lives. A door will open. A person will contact us. A new idea will be born.

Sometimes the answer will be not to take us *out* of a situation but to discover new possibilities in the old situation, or in ourselves. I knew a minister who was about to give up his profession altogether. There was no other patricular talent he discovered in himself and nothing else he deeply wanted to do, as in the case of the minister who became a financial advisor. Fortunately he took some time to pray about it and to commit the problem to the healing light of God. Within a few days he slowly realized that he had been turning himself into a kind of person he was not. He had thought he had to be a certain kind of minister: a ball-playing, church-building, committee-joining, out-with-the-young-people-roller-skating kind of pastor. He had been trying for years to make himself into an activist pillar of the community, with cheerful words and happy smiles for all occasions. But he wasn't at all that kind of person. No wonder he was exhausted. God had wanted him to be himself. God had wanted him to serve as minister in his own kind of way. It was almost pathetic to see his joy and release when he realized he could be himself. It took some courage and deliberation to discuss the matter with his church council and tell them that from now on he was going to increase his hours of study and counseling and his depth work with small groups. He served notice that he was going to serve God and the community with his own talents and not someone else's. He was guided by a deeper insight into the facts: he was to remain in his job but change his whole approach to it.

Whether we are visionaries who are granted signs and voices, or plain men and women with jobs to do and homes to run, it is the same when it comes to guidance. *It is in the facts which emerge after we turn ourselves over to him that we find guidance.*

God is real and he guides only by realities.

◆◆◆

TEN TESTS OF GUIDANCE ALONG THE WAY

But suppose we are not at the moment facing any big problem or decision? Maybe we are just living our daily lives and want to be sure we are living them according to the best plan of the Father for us. Or suppose we have already made some big choices or decisions and now want to be certain they were the right ones. Are there any sure ways by which we can tell if our present ways are leading us more fully into the abundance and joy of the Father? How can we tell if we are off the track?

There are many tests, but ten specific ones appear to me to be the most crucial as touchstones. It is my observation that they cannot be applied singly. If our course of action cannot meet the test of any one of them, it is my opinion that this course of action is suspect. Our chosen way needs prayerful reappraisal.

The first of these is the question, do we feel free or compelled? If we feel driven to some course of action, this may be a warning sign. God leaves us freedom to say no if we choose. The Holy Spirit is never rigid or compulsive and neither driving nor anxious. Our own subconscious compulsions and other lesser spirits usually make us feel unfree and compelled.

When we are counseling someone, a good way to test whether we are speaking under guidance or under our own spirit of domination or compulsion is to note a number of physical signs. Are the toes curling tensely in the shoes? Are the hands and face muscles tense? Is our breathing uneven? Do we feel pushed or anxious? If so, these may well be signs that we are not speaking to the other person in true freedom and under guidance.

Second, is there an increasing feeling of naturalness and at-homeness in our chosen course? It is quite true, as pointed out in the previous chapter, that we can't judge guidance by feelings alone. But chronic feelings —those that persist and grow over a fairly long period of time are reassuring or warning signs. If there is a persisting awkwardness, a constant sense of inner strain or of being out of place, this may be an indication that we are going against the grain. I have not observed that God's true guidance leads us to violate our own nature. In time he will change us deeply. But he leads and changes us through growing peace and naturalness.

Third, are any obvious facts being ignored? Is there a deterioration of health, for example? If organic disease is ruled out, yet chronic or increasing fatigue, digestive problems, sleeplessness, nervous symptoms, or increasing colds are involved, these are signs that we should look more closely at our way of life. We may be driving and forcing ourselves rather than letting the energy of Christ bring about the change in us. We may be crowding our energy and time too much because we think everything depends on us. Usually if we are following God's guidance, there will be an overall improvement in health.

I know a well-meaning woman who counsels many troubled and depressed people. She herself has frequent headaches and insomnia. She thinks it her duty to keep up this work, no matter how great the strain. But her deteriorating health and nervousness are facts about herself she is ignoring: facts that indicate that either this is not the right job for her, or else she is not doing it in the right way.

Or what about the facts of plain duties and responsibilities around us? As pointed out previously, a sense of duty alone is not enough to determine guidance, but if we find ourselves ignoring the fact that we have families and neighbors to cherish, feed, comfort, and counsel, we should become suspicious of our "guidance." I know a woman so deeply involved with church and community that her children feel alone, left out.

She is too busy with "good works" to sit down and be companionable.

What about the facts of the promises we have made? Promises to our marriage partner? Promises made to our children when they were baptized?

What about the facts of our real gifts, abilities, training? Are we really doing the things we can do well? Or are we chasing after an unrealistic image of ourselves?

Fourth in our touchstones of living according to God's plan is, what are the fruits, the results of our choice? Are we consistently failing? Do the people and projects we are involved with seem worse off than before? Are there genuine constructive results? The novelist Graham Greene once wrote, "Saints are always successful." That shocked me at first until I thought it over. It is true. History reveals that the saints did what they set out to do. Solid realities emerged from their convictions. They had more than visions and voices; they also had facts and evidence. Martyrdom is not a sign of failure. Quite the contrary. The only true failure is frustration and dreams unfulfilled by realities.

Too often we interpret our failures as the fault, the stubbornness, of others. But generally, a consistent failure of our project means that we are not being moved by God's own strength and timing. The first prayer group I ever led started out in a burst of enthusiasm with many eager members. But as the year went on it dwindled away, lost its fire and its members. It became a boring routine. I set my teeth, thought martyrish thoughts about my unappreciated efforts, and determined to keep on with the meetings even if I sat there alone! A wise friend, who knew a lot more about guidance than I did, suggested, "Go underground for a while. Obviously the way you're going about this is not the way God wants it done. It is not your group, you know. It is *his*. Let him show you the way." So I told the church leaders that I wanted to think over the matter for a while. Eventually, a tiny new group came to life spontaneously from the ashes of the old one. It meets quietly and has grown steadily. Men as well as women come, with six or seven denominations represented. There is no feeling of boredom or strain. We feel it is guided by Christ, not by our own well-meaning willpower.

Fifth, at this point we must ask if there is a growing ability on our part to communicate with others? Do we seem more able to reach the real thoughts and needs of other people? Or do walls seem to be growing between us and others? Often those who talk the most about the need for love and communication seem to be exactly the ones who are least aware that other people are present. So often in our enthusiasm for "causes" and justice for all, we use other human beings as objects or sounding boards. They become merely a means to our own (doubtless worthy) ends.

I knew a minister who became bitter over the attitude of one of the young women in his church. She had promised to teach in the church school, but a few days before classes began she backed out. He tried to change her mind because good teachers are hard to find. But stubbornly and irrationally she kept repeating that God had never sent her any children of her own, so obviously she would not be a fit teacher for other people's children. Instead of becoming deeply concerned over her suffering and her confusion, he left the house in resentment. He had become an organizer, angry at a worker who had let him down, rather than a pastor aware of the need of a fellow human being.

This is an extreme example, of course, of a depersonalized attitude toward others. But we are all guilty of it at times. If we find the tendency growing on us (and how hard it is to admit it!), we had better look again at our claim to guidance. When it is God who is guiding us, our loving awareness keeps pace with our enthusiasm for our ideals and goals.

Sixth, is the world around us becoming more real and significant? When we are caught by an obsession instead of being led by guidance, the world, its objects and its people become colorless and dim to us. As we grow in genuine love and guidance, the details of life become excitingly significant. Colors are brighter. Food tastes better. We are not bored. A young man I know, who is recovering from drug addiction, remarked to his parents, "Real life seems too bright." Later, he learned to love again the bright, sharp clarity of reality. As we grow in the Holy Spirit all things take on depth and brightness the way a spring morning looks after a heavy rain the night before.

Seventh, are we willing to take no for an answer? Are we able to accept it when a door closes as well as when one opens? It is a constant and insidious temptation for us to be the savior of someone whom we love. We resolve to batter down their doors and save them in spite of themselves. We have all known the kind of person of whom it is said: "She lives for others. You can tell the 'others' by the hunted look in their eyes!" An old hymn goes something like this:

> Inspire a feeble worm
> To rush into thy Kingdom, Lord,
> And take it as by storm!

But we certainly can't take the kingdom of another person by storm. When Jesus entered a town that resisted his teaching, he didn't hang around hoping to change their minds. He merely left. His departure was not made in a spirit of anger, contempt, or indifference, but rather in sorrowful recognition of another's decision. In this same spirit he accepted the decision of the rich young man to stay with his riches.

Love coming from God's guidance does not hang around another person's neck insisting on being his means of grace. Sometimes God guides us to turn away from another person's path and go about our business. We still love him. We still pray for him. We hope that someday we may be brought again into his life as an active agent. But for the present we must open our hands and let him go his own way in freedom.

The ability to discern the resistance or acceptance of another grows as we mature in Christ. But the temptation to turn ourselves into saviors also grows. We will look more deeply in a later chapter into this temptation which grows with power.

Eighth in our touchstones of living according to God's plan is, are we living a reasonably full and efficient life? It is a fairly good sign of leaving the path of guidance if we find that we have radically departed from healthy regular habits. Have we gone "lopsided"? Are we over-eating, sleeping too much, letting things like corre-spondence, studies, house-cleaning, and financial obli-gations go neglected? If we find we are letting ordinary routines and habits slide, it is generally a sign of inner conflict. It doesn't always mean the particular job or choice is wrong for us. It may mean that a destructive counterenergy has been allowed to take over. Destruc-tive or distorted energies, habits, or obsessions can swiftly destroy our integrity and energy if not swiftly committed to the restoring and purifying energy of Christ.

Ninth, have we submitted our way, our choice, to any kind of community test? It is true that sometimes we must disobey our families. Sometimes we have to disagree with our friends. Sometimes we must hold out against the opinion of our church. But we should seriously examine our claims to guidance if every com-munity which we had formerly respected is opposed, troubled, or hurt by what we do. Or if it appears that, by applying all the other tests, we still must break with our former communities, then we must try to find other groups or communities (who have

71

proved their guidance by their fruits) in whose context we can keep growing, and who will help us by praying with us, talking things over, warning us, and restoring us. We are so made that our maturing in Christ is generally necessary in a community—in some form of the "Body of Christ."

Tenth, are we becoming more aware of our dependence on Christ as we grow? When we succeed, are we increasingly aware that it is the Christ who works through us? When we fail, are we able to say matter-of-factly with Brother Lawrence, "I shall never do otherwise if I am left to myself."

It is the secret of our growing joy and power that we don't have to depend on our willpower and good intentions anymore. "No one can live as confidently as the Christian who has lost all confidence in himself. His confidence has deeper roots beyond himself." [1]

What about the guidance that comes from thoughts and convictions during quiet times, meditation, and prayer? These too, along with a sense of duty, desire, visions and voices, should be put to the tests. During quiet times of meditation much fresh inspiration often comes, but also much material from the unrecognized depths of our own personalities. God may indeed be guiding us through these means to begin with. But he will always follow up the idea, the inspiration, the conviction, with the opening doors of reality. Look at the facts of the present situation to see if we are on the

[1] James Smart, *The ABC's of Christian Faith* (Philadelphia: Westminster Press, 1968), p. 51.

72

right way; then look for the new facts that develop after prayer.

I am thinking of two examples of resistance to guidance. Two people, one who lived three hundred years ago, and another who lives today, were admired by their friends for their apparent goodness. But as we look at their lives from the point of view of the facts and realities of their situations, we may well wonder if they had completely resisted guidance while thinking they were following it.

The first of these was a French missionary priest to the Huron Indians in Canada in the seventeenth century. His name was Noel Chabanel. Deeply gifted in languages, he had been a professor of rhetoric in France. He felt called to give up his teaching post, and go into missionary work on the Canadian frontier. During his years in Canada, he met with one humiliation, obstacle, and frustration after another. In the first place, he couldn't learn the Huron language, though he was fluent in Greek, Hebrew, Italian, and Spanish. Apparently he never learned to love the life among the Huron Indians. The food, the smell, the vermin were repulsive to him the whole time. In addition to the language problem and the physical problems, he felt an almost constant spiritual desolation and homesickness. Even his ecclesiastical superiors urged him to return to France and the teaching profession to which he was so well suited.

Eventually this tormented man made a vow of perpetual stability in the Huron Missions, in order to resist the "temptation" to return. He was later killed in the Indian wars.

I read of this deeply sincere, well-meaning life with a sense of deep tragedy. He had thought he was living the life most pleasing to Christ. He had thought the more he suffered, the better his life would be. But the facts of guidance were against him the whole way. The facts of his physical, emotional, spiritual, and intellectual maladjustment were signs that he misinterpreted.

Obviously any life of dedication has some sacrifices, problems, and suffering. But a life of constant pain, a life in which every door is closed against us, in which we go downhill physically, in which we feel chronic spiritual desolation and abandonment, in which we feel no great love or attraction to our work, and which is attended by meager results or outright failure, is not the life intended for us by our Father. It was not Father Chabanel's death of martyrdom that signified his mistake. Many of the missionaries to the Hurons were likewise martyred, but their lives had been to them and to others lives of enthusiasm, fulfillment, love, accompanied by ability and the fruits of that ability.

"Let us run with perseverance the race that is set before us, looking to Jesus . . . who for the joy that was set before him endured the cross." (Hebrews 12:1-2). Any cross we embrace in which we are not aware of the joy "set before us" is not the cross given us by God. Any sacrifice he asks of us is for the sake of a greater joy, a vaster beauty, a deeper fulfillment, a more fruitful life.

74

One need not look to an example three hundred years ago to see this kind of mistake. It is a mistake perpetrated in large and small ways by just as many people today, who are sincerely trying to live a Christian life.

I know a woman who has a genuine gift for painting. She loves to paint, and others love her work. She not only has the facts of talent and love in her favor, but she also has the gift of time. Her children are now in school, and she could devote several hours a day to her work. But she feels it her duty to tie herself up completely with odd jobs, in the community, the school, the P.T.A. She says yes to every demand on her time and energy. As a result she is in a state of constant exhaustion and frustration. She feels she is living a very unselfish life in trying to make herself into the stereotype of an "active, outgoing young mother." But she is not happy or fulfilled in these jobs. She has only mediocre talent for them. She wonders why she is not happy since she is always doing her "duty." In bewilderment she has prayed about it, but then she has shut her eyes to the facts and realities of her own life. The facts are that God has given her a talent in painting and she now has the time to study it. Another fact is that her family suffers from her headaches and tensions as she rushes from one community job to another.

This is a person who believes in prayer and is bewildered that her life is an increasing burden to her. Because people think they already know what God wants of them, they sometimes close their eyes to the actual motion of his hands in their lives. He opens doors to us if we ask him to. But they are not usually the doors we have expected—and they are always doors of joy and challenge.

An old Shaker hymn goes something like this:

'Tis the gift to be simple, 'tis the gift to be free.
'Tis the gift to come down where we ought to be.
And when we find ourselves in the place just right,
'Twill be in the valley of love and delight.

This sums up extremely well the nature of guidance and the God who guides us.

There is another point about guidance I have recently observed. As a man or woman grows in Christ, there is less and less coincidence in his life. Those I have known who have gone most deeply into prayer and dependence on Christ's energy say that more and more the random, the coincidental, and the accidental events seem to drop out of their lives. They discover that the exchange of glances with a stranger is a call to prayer for that stranger; the random thought of someone, the telephone call, and the letter received all come for a purpose.

I personally have not yet reached this point. There is still, for most of us, a great deal of material in our lives and minds which is not yet under the full control of Christ. Though we have given ourselves to him and his flag is planted in the surrendered territory, there are still many pockets of resistance, destructiveness, and

76

fear. Though in essence we are already a "new creation" we are not yet completely changed into his likeness. His energy does not yet flow unimpeded.

This is nothing to be anxious or guilty about. But we must attempt to understand our remaining random or demonic thoughts. Most of us blunder into accidents and temptations occasionally. Often we find ourselves taking burdens which are not God's will for us, or answering calls which are not our calling. But as we grow, we will find that things become less unconnected and inconsequential. There will be less static and less wire-crossing in our lives. All the small and large things in our lives will gradually become purposeful and sacramental.

We cannot push this growth. But we can pray for it, and expect it eagerly. As Christ possesses us and changes us, he also comes to possess the events in our lives.

GROWING IN DARKNESS

Just before I sat down to write this chapter tonight there came a phone call from a young man whom I have sometimes counseled. He had been showing a genuine interest in growing in prayer and had begun to respond to God with great vitality.

"It all suddenly seems so unreal," he said on the telephone. "All the spark and the enthusiasm have left. I can't feel *anything*, except depression and fatigue. I call out and there is just silence around me; and there does not seem any sense in being alive. What am I doing wrong? Why is God doing this to me?"

Sooner or later most of us will go through this kind of experience as we grow. With some of us it may not be as intense a depression as this student was feeling. And it may come in different ways. But usually it has the same identifying signs: an inner fatigue, a lethargy, a boredom with the very thought of God or prayer, a creeping anxiety and weakness. Sometimes it comes swiftly. Sometimes it surrounds us slowly and insidiously like fingers of a thick fog. In whatever way it comes, God seems unreal and far away, and prayer seems not only powerless, but a great strain.

The world around us—people and things—seems dimmer and rather indistinct. The grass is not as green as it used to be. Little annoying habits and temptations seem stronger. We are theoretically aware of the great richness and potentialities of life, but a sort of inner paralysis grips us. We are like a man fainting with exhaustion, who looks with indifference at a gold mine. Yes, we feel that all that richness is there for us to take, but we cannot do anything about it. It is too much of an effort. At this point we feel as Job did:

> Behold, I go forward, but he is not there;
>   and backward, but I cannot perceive him;
> on the left hand I seek him, but I cannot
>   behold him;
> I turn to the right hand, but I cannot see him. . . .
> God has made my heart faint . . .
> for I am hemmed in by darkness,
>   and thick darkness covers my face.
> (Job 23:8-9, 16-17)

79

This experience comes to most of us somewhere along the line as we grow spiritually. Perhaps it may come several times. But before we can consider what to do at these times, we must try to find out *why* it comes.

I do not believe that God sends this experience any more than he sends physical illness. He does not want or will it. He is neither punishing nor testing us. His deepest will is that we always feel his nearness, his joy, and his strength.

So why do this inner fatigue and darkness strike almost inevitably? One of the great mystics of our century, Evelyn Underhill, explains what is going on in a significant way:

The dark night, then, is really a deeply human process in which the self which thought itself so spiritual, so firmly established upon the supersensual plane is forced to turn back, to leave the light, and pick up those qualities which it had left behind. Only thus, by the transmutation of the *whole* man, not by a careful and departmental cultivation of that which we like to call his "spiritual side" can divine humanity be formed.[1]

In other words, this inner fatigue, lethargy, or boredom we experience is brought on by overstraining, emphasizing certain things at the expense of others, ignoring certain facts in the situation, and depending too much on our own willpower and good intentions.

[1] Evelyn Underhill, *Mysticism* (New York: Noonday Press), p. 388.

Growing in Darkness

I went on a "health" diet once without consulting a doctor first. I thought I was progressing very well. But as the weeks and months went on I began to develop strange shooting pains throughout my body. I developed a slight tremor of the hands and a tingling or numb sensation in the hands and feet. I felt tired all the time. Finally I consulted the doctor. He examined me and looked at me grimly saying, "You have a severe vitamin deficiency. If you had kept on this way you would have gone into beriberi!"

My situation was very similar to that of the spiritual enthusiast who has not sought wise guidance. We overshoot the mark. We rush up certain paths completely ignoring the obvious ones. Perhaps we are ignoring the presence of some destructive feeling of resentment or self-pity. Perhaps we are overemphasizing hours of meditation at the expense of work with the hands. Perhaps we are counseling beyond our depth. Perhaps we are so emphasizing intercessory prayer that we leave no room for adoring or enjoying God. Perhaps we are working beyond the limits of our genuine love without the help of prayer.

A young man I know threw himself into fine work for racial justice in the ghettos of the city, denying himself quiet times for thought or relaxation. Recently he came to a counselor's office and broke into sobs, "I've been giving, and giving, and giving. Why doesn't someone give to *me* for a change?"

The inner fatigue and darkness mean that we have been ignoring some aspect of God's will for us to be-

81

long to him *wholly,* not just in part. It need not be a deadly illness. We can learn from it. But just how do we keep growing when almost paralyzed by such a condition?

In the first place, tell the truth about it to yourself. Do not pretend you are full of faith, fervor, and enthusiasm when you are not. There is nothing more deadly than self-deception in this matter. Admit in prayer that you do feel darkened, at a standstill, empty. Do not telephone all your friends and make them listen to a detailed description of this inner darkness, but *do* tell at least one trusted friend who has some experience in the matter, or one small, understanding, and experienced group.

Not everyone knows how to receive someone else's honesty about his own feelings. I was with a group once in which a young man confessed his deep anxieties about his wife and her emotional breakdown. He said her doctor was pessimistic. The young man said he believed God could help, but still he just couldn't help being worried. Instantly one of the enthusiasts replied, "Oh, you mustn't feel that way!" and proceeded to give him a rousing lecture on how he *ought* to be feeling. This was an extremely destructive response. The first rule of receiving someone else's honest confession is *never* tell him he must *not* feel that way. He *does* feel that way. He wouldn't be talking about it if he could snap out of it by his own willpower. All this woman did was to add a feeling of guilt to the young

82

man's already intense feelings of anxiety. All she did was to place on him the extra burden of pretending to himself and to the group that he felt differently.

We trust that our feeling will eventually change under the guidance of Christ. But first it must be faced with honesty. It will certainly not change if driven underground. It will only become more subtly destructive. God knows all about it already. We can't put on any act for him. We often try, of course, to put on "stained-glass" attitudes and impress him with our endurance, but he sees right through it!

Try to keep calm about your feelings. Most of us have these experiences from time to time. It does not mean that we have committed the unforgivable sin. It does not mean that God will never seem close again. It is a condition that Christ will heal. He is stronger and more real than our temporary feeling or nonfeeling about him.

Try to find out what you are neglecting or straining in yourself that brought about the condition, but don't try to fight, or force an immediate change. The system must be healed first. You can face the cause of your painful dryness, place it in the hands of God, ask for whatever changes you need to begin in you. We must remain alert and receptive to new possibilities and open doors before us. Some small acts may be suggested to us as we try out new ways, but it may take a while for the feelings to be healed and restored.

While keeping alert to new possibilities that God may

be bringing into our lives, we shouldn't make any major changes in our pattern of life while this condition lasts. This is not the time for us to decide to leave our jobs, leave college, get a divorce, or get married. Pain or numbness can play queer tricks on us. It is usually *small* (though significant) changes that God asks of us at these times. When we are healed, and the energies start flowing through us again, then we may be guided to make some major changes.

One should live as simply and healthfully as possible during these times. Physically, it is a time to eat less, but have better-balanced meals, drink more water, and be disciplined about hours of rest. Spiritually, it is a time to increase simple relaxed thanksgiving and trustful looking towards God, who holds us even though we cannot feel him. When counseling or praying for others at these times, it is important to let the Christ do the carrying. We can pray silently, even while with another person: "I am confused and tired. I don't know how to help this person. Just use me as your channel and reach this person, even though I cannot." The prayer of tired trustfulness is a prayer of great power, because our own energies and enthusiasms are not getting in the way of what God wants for the other person.

In cases of extreme inner fatigue we can just commit our whole prayer list to Christ, and for several days refrain from specifically praying for anyone at all. We can ask a friend or a prayer group to carry us and our concerns while we are renewed.

While we are being healed is a good time to emphasize small, symbolic acts of obedience and readiness. It is interesting to see in the Gospels how often Jesus asked the person he was healing or helping to do some small physical act. It seems to serve in a similar way to the cork being drawn out of the bottle, enabling new energy to flow forth. For example, if the housewife, when facing an active day of cleaning or mending or ironing, feels overwhelmed with lethargy and asks God to send her the strength, often she will find that the strength does not flow through her until she actually picks up the broom, after praying.

As a writer, often I have to ask for strength to keep on writing. But frequently I feel no strength returning until I sit at the typewriter and write the first word, after praying. When we have been angry with someone, and have prayed for the lifting of that darkness, the restoration of the relationship, often the prayed-for healing does not flow through until we have reached out a hand and touched the person, or done him a small service of some kind. This is not an earning of God's help. Rather, it is a releasing or uncorking act of obedience and relinquishment, which is a symbolic way of saying yes to the help he already offers. This is a most important thing to remember when in this paralyzing darkness. Choose little ways, physical ways, of saying yes to the God who is healing us.

"It is expedient for thee to flee to humble and outward works, and to refresh thyself with good actions, to await with a firm confidence my coming,"

85

Thomas à Kempis tells us, in *Imitation of Christ.* Such outwardness relaxes us into the hands of God.

But what about the times of acute darkness? Not the slowly creeping fog of fatigue and dimness of soul, but some sharp overwhelming emotion that temporarily wipes out everything else? How can one keep a hold on God and keep growing while this emotion is shaking his foundations?

Take pain, for example. One of my closest friends was a woman extremely ill with cancer. She had trained herself in the discipline of positive thinking and firm affirmation. But sometimes, she told me, the pain became so great that her affirmations and courageous will didn't seem to help. I told her that at times of great pain we should not strain ourselves with the resistance of reason. At such times we should surrender ourselves like a child into the hands of the Savior, not straining upward, but letting his strong compassionate strength reach out to us. It is not we who by our faith and strength hold on to him, but rather he who keeps his hold on us. Call on him, and lean on him trustfully, knowing he has not sent us this pain, and is willing to release us from it. If we cannot pray, we can repeat inwardly some scriptural phrase that helps us, such as: "Around us are the everlasting arms." We should not be too shy to ask the help of a prayer group at such times.

In our daily lives, before any serious illnesses or accidents come, we should practice with *little* pains that come our way. When we stub our toe, or burn our finger, or bump our head, we should learn how to turn the injury and pain *instantly* over to Christ, even before we say "ouch." Literally, it cuts the pain in half; because, when we do this, the body relaxes its instinctive resistance and tension, and healing forces are allowed to flow through. When we learn to do this in little things, it becomes an instinctive thing to do when greater crises come.

What about fear? Fear is the most paralyzing of all emotions of darkness, especially when it touches on some phobia. It is a most destructive emotion, but far too often spiritual advice just increases its destructiveness by making us dread it too much. We are told so often that we should not give in to fear—that it puts up a block between us and God and destroys the power of faith—that we make the mistake of concentrating on not having fear. Naturally that just increases its power over us. It reminds me of our childhood recipe for making gold: "Stir half a pound of salt and sugar in a quart of water for half an hour—without *once* thinking of the word 'hippopotamus.' "

To overcome the destructive power of fear, we must first admit to ourselves that we are afraid. Then we can affirm that, afraid though we are, Christ is stronger than our fear. Then we can turn ourselves, including our fear, over to him. Let him have the courage for us. Let him do all the positive thinking for us. Our weakness and fear won't stop his work through us if we keep turning that weakness over to him to deal with, instead of trying to wrestle with it ourselves. Even if there is only a tiny amount of trust and faith in us, that is enough for him to work with. The Bible is full of examples of how the power of God can take a "little thing, trustfully offered," and do great things with it: the mustard seed, the bit of yeast in the loaf, the widow's pennies, the few loaves and fish offered by the boy to Jesus, the jug of water at the wedding feast. We offer the vehicle, the channel; God does all the rest.

But what will he do exactly, when we admit the fear and turn it over to him? Much of my thinking these days is centered around the ninety-first Psalm, and the problems its assertions pose for those who know something about the actual state of the world.

He who dwells in the shelter of the Most High . . .
will say to the Lord . . .
   "my God, in whom I trust."
For he will deliver you from the snare of
      the fowler
   and from the deadly pestilence . . .
You will not fear the terror of the night,
   nor the arrow that flies by day,
nor the pestilence that stalks in darkness,
   nor the destruction that wastes at noonday.

You will tread on the lion and the adder,
   the young lion and the serpent you will trample
      under foot.

Because he cleaves to me in love, I will deliver him;
   I will protect him . . .

88

When he calls to me, I will answer him;
I will be with him in trouble,
I will rescue him and honor him.

I used to refuse to repeat this psalm in church because it seemed wrong to me to make such statements, even from the Bible, when they didn't fit the facts. How could I believe these sweeping promises of security when millions of righteous people had been destroyed?

But now I am not so sure. I have begun to think this bold and challenging psalm is speaking the straight facts of what the world could be like, and *will* be like when we are fully cooperating with spiritual laws. It is a vision of the world as God intended it. It is not enough to *mean* well. We must learn wisdom and union with the healing energies of creation. This ninety-first Psalm is saying something about the profound laws built into the very structure of the universe by a God who has not willed tragedy or disease upon us. This psalm describes what almost every one of us has experienced occasionally: some kind of inexplicable healing and protection which arose from a depth beyond our own. It shows that God has not intended man to be a driven, frightened, sick, and helpless animal. It describes how life would be for us if we had learned the wisdom of union with God's intention. It shows a life in which we have become the master over matter, because we have become so completely the child of God.

This has already happened in the lives of some people. There are some men and women who seem largely immune to the accidents, diseases, and decay which plague the rest of us. They are not hiding in ivory towers. They live vigorously and daringly in the world. But somehow they have become one with the deep rhythm of God and are quite literally dwelling "in the shelter of the Most High" even when active in this material dimension.

God is not playing favorites. He is not breaking laws of nature for them. Rather, he is able to fulfill his deepest laws through them. In them we see what he has intended for all men.

But notice an important thing about the ninety-first Psalm. Even in the state of security the potential danger is not taken away! The terror by night, the arrow by day, the pestilence in the darkness, the destruction at noonday, the lion, the serpent, though they will not harm us, they are nevertheless *there*. God has not promised to take us out of a universe with the potentialities for evil and pain. Otherwise, there would be no free will. As he answers our prayer for release from fear, he will definitely not put us in a cosmic padded cell where nothing will threaten us. The thing we are frightened of may be permitted to remain in our path, staring at us. But his strength will enable us to walk up to it, look at it, and go on past it. It cannot overcome us.

It is wise to practice this with little fears: how will we pay the doctor? Why didn't the children telephone? What about the promotion? When we commit the little fears to him, it will become instinctive to do

90

the same with the big crises that come. Eventually, fear will no longer be the smothering, crippling thing it used to be. It is true that feelings take a long time to change. But as pointed out in the chapter on guidance, we must look to results and facts, not feelings. A letter came from a girl not long ago who has long been in the grip of compulsive anxiety. Recently she turned her life over to God for the first time. She is concerned because a lot of fear and anxiety persist in spite of her conversion. Did that mean, she wondered, that she hadn't really given herself to God? Or did it mean that he couldn't really change her?

This was a puzzler for a while. We couldn't figure out either why she was still in a pit of fear. But then, as we thought it over, we realized that the facts of her life *had* changed, even though her feelings had not. She could make friends now far more easily. Communication flowed more freely. She could express herself as she had not been able to before. She was able to hold down an excellent research job now. Several people had already been greatly helped by her. She was, in short, not at all the same person she had been five years before. The facts of her personality and her life were profoundly different. The center of her life had indeed been taken over by Christ.

She was like a person who puts himself into the hands of a surgeon. After the operation is over and the growth has been removed, uncomfortable feelings may remain for quite a while. But the basic problem has been corrected. The person is moving towards health now, and can afford to take in stride the temporarily lingering discomfort. That too will someday be overcome. The fact is that the patient is cured.

"Those who have the wind of the Holy Spirit, go forward, even in sleep," wrote Brother Lawrence centuries ago. And this is the secret of continuing to grow even when apparently paralyzed by the darkness of fear, pain, or lethargy. However the condition may have come about, God continues to heal us, change us, and draw us toward joy. He may be working on such deep subconscious levels of our being that we feel nothing. We don't feel the X-rays as they penetrate to the deep tissues of the body and change them. Or we are maybe only conscious of holding to his reality blindly, without joy or radiance at the moment. In any case, it is enough.

I visited a woman who was having a severe nervous breakdown. "I'm aware all the time of God," she told me. I asked her if she meant she was aware of comfort or joy or hopefulness. "No," she answered. "I don't feel those things. Just God. There is darkness all around me, but he's right here with me in this darkness. Just God."

There is no "outside" of God. There is no way of not being enclosed by him. When I used to climb mountains in the West, I often came to bare spots: places where no trees or grass was growing. But all the time I was aware of the mountain itself under my feet. Its reality was holding me up, no matter what surface bareness I was experiencing.

God does not send darkness, dryness, or bareness. It has come because in some way (as an individual or as a part of humanity) we have resisted healthy growth. Nevertheless, perhaps the greatest experience of growth possible can come from this experience, because we learn how, for the first time, to lean *only* on the fact of his unadorned reality. And when the light and the joy return—which they will—that bare fact of his reality under our feet holding us up will remain the main source of our joy. "By this we shall . . . reassure our hearts before him whenever our hearts condemn us; for God is greater than our hearts."

(1 John 3:19-20)

PROBLEMS OF POWER

"He who is near me is near the fire," Jesus is quoted as saying in one of the apocryphal discourses. As we pray and grow, we realize his is not only the fire of compassionate love, but also the fire of power.

And power can be used destructively. There is much wisdom in the myth of Lucifer, the great angel of light. He was so powerful, gifted, and beautiful that when he rebelled against the Father the damage he did was far greater than if he had been a less advanced spirit.

Of course we have seen this in our own generation and civilization. The very powers and techniques we have developed to solve our problems have opened the possibilities of even graver problems.

The more we receive God's power into our life, the more harm we will do if we try to use this power independently of him. Jesus' temptation in the wilderness was no empty show. He must have known, even in early life, that his powers were far beyond those of ordinary men. He must have begun to realize that his powers were stronger than time, space, and matter. He knew the incredible control he could exercise over the will and imaginations of other men. How was he going to use this power? This may well have been for him a more agonizing struggle and decision than the one later in Gethsemane.

It upsets some Christians to be warned about this. We like to think that our growing is going to be smooth. We don't like to face the fact that we will be tempted. It horrifies us to realize that even after belonging to Christ we are capable not only of doing harm to others, but of doing much greater harm than before. But we are not playing games as we go into the fire of Christ. We are moving into a dimension of tremendous forces. There is nothing to fear if we are—to use the scriptural phrase—"strong in the Lord." There is everything to fear if we, like Lucifer, try to become that source of strength ourselves.

One of the greatest of these problems is apt to arise through our growing sensitivity to other people. We are growing in love. People *matter* to us now. It becomes natural to involve ourselves with their needs. This is a wonderful way to grow. But if we forget that we are only a branch of Christ the vine, and not the vine itself, we will also grow in fatigue and strain.

This can do terrible things to our physical and emotional health. When Christ changes us, he enlarges our capacities of awareness and response, so he can work through us more fully. Our whole body-mind complex becomes energized, sensitized, and awakened. Like precision instruments we are changed to register the slightest need of others. *We have become far more powerful and, at the same time, far more dependent!*

If we forget our dependence, and are only aware of our power, if we try to love others and change situations by our own strength alone, then our sensitive awareness can become dangerous to us.

A few years back, I was trying to help a group of people who were deeply involved in painful problems. I had been changed a little bit by Christ and led into a greater concern than I would have ordinarily felt. I listened and talked with them. I sat up half the night with them, and during the day surrendered most of my privacy. During the times I was alone, I carried their burdens on my mind. But this kind of burden can be shouldered only with deep and constant prayer. When taking up this kind of cross, we must turn hourly to God, from whom all energy flows.

But I forgot to pray. I tried to carry it all myself. In short, I began demanding of my body and mind what God *never* demands—that I love and serve my brother 100 percent by my own system alone. And of course that system underwent grave strain. For a long time,

96

I ignored the growing fatigue and tension as unworthy of my notice; but I couldn't ignore the eventual explosion of unreasonable temper and the physical illness that followed! Most of us kindergarten Christians could tell a similar story about ourselves.

A growing perfectionism and chronic guilt are other real problems. As it says in *The Imitation of Christ:* "The higher a person has advanced in the Spirit, so much heavier are the crosses he often finds, because the grief of his banishment increases with his love to God." As we become more aware and honest we see ourselves as never before. And often we are appalled!

A certain amount of this leads to healthy confession. Christ can't change us much until we learn at least a little about where we are blocking him. But then we have to go on from there in trust, increased prayer, and with a little ironic humor as we see our own finiteness and foolishness.

But some Christians stay at the point of guilt. They become grim and anxious perfectionists. Long anxiety over mistakes and chronic self-contempt over failure can turn their prayer into a tense and joyless affair. The Christian life becomes a burden to them, not a release.

The wise mystic Molinos once wrote: "He that rises again quickly and continues the race is as if he had never fallen." The best way to rise and continue is to pray with frankness and cheerfulness, "Lord, that's the way I am and the way I act when I don't let you help me!" and then simply turn ourselves over to him all

97

over again, asking for the strength to do better next time.

One of the most troublesome problems of power is what monastics sometimes call "inordinate affections." As we grow in the love of others, sometimes that love becomes emotional obsession. This is nothing to be ashamed of, but it *is* something to watch for. Our awareness of the lovableness of others, particularly the opposite sex, is a beautiful gift of the Father. It is part of being a full and growing human being. But we mustn't fool ourselves if our loving desire to help drifts over into romantic dreams. I have known of more than one sexual affair developing out of this kind of self-deception, in which the Christian thought his passionate attraction to another was only on a "spiritual" level.

We should take a long level look at our emotions, accepting the fact that we are a human male or female and that God has made us so as part of the beauty of life. And then we must turn these feelings over to the Father, praying him not to *lessen* our ability to love but to *increase* it, so we can go beyond obsession with just one person and lovingly serve many. This energy, thus accepted and committed, can be firmly directed in more creative and appropriate channels. It need be neither suppressed on the one hand, nor allowed to become a central obsession on the other.

More insidious than romantic obsession, and less hard to identify, is our frequent desire to make other people dependent on us. In our growing compassionate eagerness to serve, we often hope the other person will

98

increasingly look to *us* as the source of help and loving power. We realize (with secret joy) that the other person is turning to us as we would turn to God, and is literally praying to us, according to the deepest meaning of prayer.

When this happens we are tempted to keep the worship for ourselves, to keep the offered energy and return it with energy of our own, and thus to set up a personal relationship, rather than a mediating relationship. Anybody who has ever counseled another knows how easily this can happen. Either we will try, then, to change the other person according to our own ideas and will, or we will try to keep him in a relationship with us to feed our own needs. Thus freedom is destroyed. Thus the redemptive power Christ offers through us is short-circuited. Instead of allowing the other person to be drawn into the releasing energy of Christ, we draw him instead into our ego-centered vortex.

An elderly woman once told me what a shock it was to her to realize that a young friend she had been helping and counseling over a long period of time had overcome her worst problems and had grown into independence. The older woman had genuinely wished at first to help her young friend, but, later on, also genuinely enjoyed the feeling of being needed. She enjoyed the drama and the sense of power of being a pillar of strength to a weak person. When her friend grew out of her weakness, the counselor (who honestly faced her feelings) had to cope with a strong regret at being out of a job.

It deeply shames a strong, loving person to face the fact that he has tried to be God to another person, and thus has become a Lucifer—with all Lucifer's special power, attraction, and possessiveness. Perhaps the greatest harm we can do is to turn another person into an emotional cripple while we become an emotional vampire.

Some people fight it mistakenly—as they fight sexual awareness—by clamming up and refusing to extend themselves to others because they fear the potential dangers of this kind of energy-giving. But this is not the way. *The Father of Christ is not a God of repression, but a God of radiant abundance.* He didn't bring us out of our dark shell so that we might go right back into it out of fear of what might happen in the light. The answer is to face *all* energies, and then give them to Christ to direct. He will know what to do with them.

For example, when we sit and talk with another person who is needing help we will soon become aware of an almost electrc flow of energy back and forth. It is almost a palpable bond of need and response. When we feel this beginning to happen we must inwardly relax, let go. Picture, if it is helpful, the Christ standing behind you offering his healing through the channel of your relaxed body and mind. Accept the expression of need flowing toward you from the other person, but then picture it flowing *through and past you*—on to the Christ who stands behind you. Then picture the healing

100

energy flowing from that Christ, again through you, to the other person. See yourself as a mediator, not a source. This does not have to be explained to the other person, nor does it need interfere at all with your intent listening to him. It certainly does not mean that you are becoming cold, detached, or impervious to his need. Quite the contrary. Your own warmth and giving will also be released more fully. But it will not be a greedy, possessive warmth. It will be the warm love which releases but does not possess. The person in need will be aware not only of your warmth, but also of your freedom, and will be encouraged to reach for his own freedom.

This kind of mental picturing is helpful to some. For others it is sufficient during an interview to pray silently, "He is yours, Christ. He is really seeking you, whether he realizes it or not. You love him more than I do. You understand him as I cannot. You alone know what he needs. I am turning over to you what he is offering to me." Then we move not back, but on, into a deeper dimension of love and service than we have ever known.

What about the problem of loyalty that turns into idolatry? Paul Tournier, the Swiss psychiatrist and Christian leader, warns us somewhere that the thing that once liberated us can turn into the very thing that enslaves us. A method of prayer, a technique of meditation, a way of expressing ourselves through art, music, writing, or speaking, which was once the channel through which God reached us, may have become the thing that keeps us from continued growth. *We have confused the channels of God with God himself.* This turns us into idolators of a certain system. We become fixed and petrified. It is natural to be thrilled with each new level of growth and each new channel of inspiration, and we are apt to think, "I have arrived. This is the ultimate answer for me. I do not have to change anymore. I have grown up." But God, the living God, keeps breaking the old molds. He constantly enlarges us, presenting new challenges and new sacraments.

What is God trying to teach me *right now?* Does he want me to try group prayer as well as individual prayer? Does he want me to grow more deeply in quiet adoration? Is he asking me to use my hands for a change? Should I learn a new way of releasing myself to God and other people through dancing, art, or writing? Should I dig into an intellectual search for my faith? Is there another kind of aid to worship, another symbol, which would be helpful to me? A new kind of book to read?

We can't always decide for ourselves in which ways we are to grow and develop. As with all guidance, we must look to the actual facts and realities that develop in our situation after prayer. But with all assurance, we know there will be new ways. To hold possessively and exclusively to any one power, gift, or aid is a great obstacle to our growth.

There is another problem of power which is difficult to write about, because many readers will think it outrageously superstitious. But actually it is not so strange, once we admit that *thought* is a great power. A fact that slowly emerges, after some years of growing in prayer, is that thoughts and intentions can be used harmfully as well as helpfully. Probably our power of thought is the strongest, most basic thing about us. We have seen the limitless good that can be done in the world when we surrender this power to God through prayer. But if we choose *not* to surrender it, discipline it, or commit it to the supreme thought of God, we probably do far more harm through this power than through any other.

It is probably the observation of this fact that lies at the roots of the various witchcraft cults through history. There is a grain of truth in the center of most heresies, cults, or superstitions, or they wouldn't keep reappearing in all centuries and cultures.

But one doesn't need to draw pentagrams on the floor, kill a white rooster, or stick pins in a wax doll to harm another person. I talked to a woman recently who spoke of her cousin. She had always been outwardly kind to that cousin, and had never spoken ill of her, at least in my hearing. But, suddenly, her eyes narrowed and she said softly, "How I hate her. Nobody knows how I hate her. I always have!" She was not facing the fact of her hatred with sorrow or asking God to heal it. She was gloating over it, as if the hatred were a precious plant she had cherished for years. Obviously this hatred had harmed her in many ways. We are always being warned about the physical and emotional damage such a harbored emotion can do us. But if we

103

admit that thought is a great power, can we seriously think that it did not also do harm to the cousin? Especially if the cousin had not learned how to defend herself spiritually? It is my opinion that our cherished, malevolent thoughts can add to the burdens of others, can increase their darkness, make it harder for them to love others, and make it more difficult for them to throw off physical disease or despondency. In short, these thoughts feed poison into the mainstream of their lives.

This is particularly true if we have already become a powerful person through prayer, and then have temporarily turned away from prayer. The Father takes great risks when he lets us grow in the Spirit and share so deeply in his creative powers. For then our tempers, when we have them, do more damage. Our lust is more corrosive. Our possessiveness becomes strangling. Our scorn and contempt become fierce, cutting weapons.

Matthew tells how Jesus warned us against the misuse of our growing powers: "Whoever is angry with his brother shall be liable to judgment. Whoever says 'you fool' shall be liable to the hell of fire. Everyone who looks on a woman lustfully has already committed adultery . . . in his heart. Love your enemies. . . . Do not be anxious about your life. . . . Judge not. . . ." Surely Jesus was thinking not only of the destructive effect such deep-rooted thoughts can have on us, but also of the effect they can have on others through us. The swift, passing anger, scorn, lust, or fear, will do

104

no harm if faced and committed to Christ. It is the *welcomed, chronic* thought that starts to destroy.

As we become aware that we influence others to good or evil by our thoughts, we also become aware that others can influence us. Even when we pray for someone, it is quite possible to get sucked down into his darkness. It is a grim thought. I wish I could believe along with some of my friends that anyone who engages in any kind of prayer is automatically safe. But I am afraid I cannot. The evidence does not point that way. The Scriptures warn us explicitly that in this world we are in a war. When we are given to Christ, we take a stand against all that destroys, pulls down, and eats away. When we pray for another, we put ourselves right into the midst of conflicting forces. If we do this without putting ourselves first under Christ's protection, and attempt to use only our own powers, we are in a position (spiritually) similar to that of one who walks unarmed at night in the slums, or goes into an area of building demolition without a helmet on.

Paul meant it when he warned, "We are not contending against flesh and blood, but against the principalities, against the powers, against the world rulers of this present darkness, against the spiritual hosts of wickedness in heavenly places" (Eph. 6:12). That is what we are doing when we pray.

This is not a theory I dreamed up myself. In fact, I don't like it at all. For a long time I resisted understanding what the Scriptures were talking about in such passages. But I slowly discovered this truth by

105

observation. I began to notice that often well-balanced, healthy people would go through strange spells of gloom, fatigue, or fear for no apparent reason. As we talked about it, it would emerge that they had been expending a lot of emotional and spiritual energy interceding for someone else in emotional illness or darkness. Usually these intercessors had forgotten to put themselves under protection of Christ. I cannot prove cause and effect here. There may be all kinds of other psychological reasons which explain it. But it is something I have repeatedly noticed in both myself and others who have undertaken intercessory prayer, and I pass on the observation for what it is worth. There is nothing here to scare anyone away from intercessory prayer. The same passage in Ephesians which warns us that anyone who prays is engaged in spiritual warfare also tells us exactly how to protect ourselves. I cannot improve on it:

"Finally be strong in the Lord and in the strength of his might. Put on the whole armor of God . . . . that you may be able to withstand in the evil day, and having done all, to stand. Stand therefore, having girded your loins [another way of saying 'pull on your trousers'] with truth, . . . and having shod your feet with the equipment of the gospel of peace; above all taking the shield of faith . . . . And take the helmet of salvation, and the sword of the Spirit . . . . Pray at all times in the Spirit . . . . keep alert . . . making supplication for all the saints [that is, keep praying for others also involved in this warfare of prayer]. . . ." (Eph. 6:10-18)

106

Please take this advice quite literally. God has sent you with power into a perilous world, and when you pray, you are in the most perilous part. Put yourself deliberately under the protection of Christ!

And when we are aware of thoughts, obsessions, and wishes of our own that might feed poison into the life-streams of others, we can protect them in the same way we protect ourselves from this poison: by relinquishing them into the hands of Christ. The more obsessive the poisonous thought is, the more completely it should be surrendered to Christ to deal with. Then, in his hands, it will not be permitted to harm others.

For example, I knew a man deeply engaged in church work and the ministry of prayer who frequently counseled a married couple who were having problems. He soon became aware that he was having strong obsessive and romantic thoughts about the wife. There was no question of his telling her about it or trying to break up their marriage, and at first he thought his daydreams would do no harm. He told me he talked it over with another counselor more experienced in prayer than he, and slowly he realized that thought does not stop in the mind of the thinker. It was quite possible (in the vast subconscious union that we all have with each other) that his encouraged thoughts might indeed add a strain and tension to that marriage without anyone knowing why. By his outwardly expressed wisdom, his acts, his friendship, he was helping pull their marriage together; but by the unseen power of his thoughts he was, with equal vigor, pulling them apart.

What to do? Was he to pretend he didn't feel what he did? Should he punish himself with guilt feelings and confessions to everyone? He took a simpler, yet more drastic, way. Every time he felt his desire for the woman he prayed silently: "Lord, you know my feelings. They are very strong. I don't know how to handle them. I give this powerful emotion for you to deal with. You take it, use it, keep it from harming me, and keep it from harming my friends. Turn it to something creative for all of us." He prayed this, knowing *the God who gives the power is also stronger than the power*. The same thing can be done with powerful hatred. The same thing can be done with anxiety. *Any* feeling which may harm others can be rendered harmless through this prayer of relinquishment.

This is not an easy prayer to pray. Simple, yes, but fantastically difficult to pray. To look at a deeply rooted feeling and then tell God you are willing for him to do what he wants with it—destroy it, change it, divert it— this is a radical operation! Our whole possessive, indulgent nature rises up in protest. We'd rather fight it with our own weak wills, for though we would probably not succeed, we could always say, "I tried, but it was just too strong for me." But deep inside, we know if a feeling is given to God it will not be too strong for us. And we will be changed.

This is not intended to be a chapter of gloom. These warnings need cause no one hesitation in giving himself to growth and power. Once we have learned that "the greatest temptations are on the steps of the altar," as

108

C. S. Lewis has said, we are forewarned. We know now that our change into people of greater power does not ensure our automatic good influence. We learn that every vigorous, deep, and cultivated thought of good or evil, love or malice, is busily at work in someone's life at this very moment. We learn that with Christ, our powers grow. If we turn away from him, our problems grow apace.

This need not make us afraid. It need only make us realize how much we need him!

POSSIBLE PSYCHIC DEVELOPMENTS IN PRAYER

Sooner or later we will have to face it. Almost inevitably some kind of psychic or extrasensory awareness develops as the Christian grows. Many people consider this to be a real problem of power. Others consider it an exciting challenge. In any case, this is certainly a problem chapter, because it digs into an issue widely misunderstood on the one hand, and widely misused on the other. If the subject of guidance disturbs some people, that of psychic phenomena throws them into fits!

Nevertheless, something *must* be said. And we must say it as Christians and church members. There's plenty being said, both intelligent and otherwise, outside church circles. From book stalls, newspaper reports, television interviews, parapsychological laboratories, we hear constantly of the strange bewildering powers of the human mind and its relation to the invisible realities and energies around us. Perhaps we dismiss it all as the merest nonsense or evidence of mass psychosis; and then along comes some personal, authentic experience that we cannot explain or dismiss.

What can the intelligent Christian think? Where can he go for guidance and explanation? Will the church help him? I have never yet heard a sermon anywhere that attempted to think through and interpret the psychic experience to Christians. As far as I know, no theological seminary offers a course on this subject, though they offer a wide variety of other courses relating theology to all other aspects of life and growth. Although the subject has such astounding implications for theology and faith, for some reason it has become a hushed-up matter among theologians and church leaders. I don't know why. We are as ignorant, scared, and secretly fascinated by it as Victorians ever were by sex. It is the scientists (the physicists, psychologists, anthropologists) and the philosophers who have spearheaded the investigations and written the important books, recorded experimentation, and documented evidence.

Parapsychology, now about a century old, is still an infant science. Psychic phenomena, of course, have been occurring, apparently, since the beginning of recorded history, but only in the last hundred years has there been a serious, organized attempt to investigate

111

the material too often brushed aside as individual or group delusion, folktales, or mythology. Anyone who cares to read, with an open and inquiring mind, the Proceeds of the American and British Societies of Psychical Research, will find that there is plenty of good evidence that our abilities of mind and thought far transcend the limitations of time, space, and the five senses. There is evidence to be had, far exceeding our own personal experiences, that there are dimensions of reality around us, usually invisible to us, with which we communicate and interact. If this does not have profound theological implications, then nothing does!

Psychic experience is a real though small part of our general spiritual development. I have never yet met a person who has gone deeply and faithfully into prayer who has not eventually had some growing psychic awareness to report.

Its development sometimes comes as a shock. But actually it is a natural part of life and growth. Through prayer we have already learned that there are many mysteries unfolding in God's universe. As we become sensitively aware of all aspects of life—beauty, suffering, love, other people, our own selves—so we also become more sensitively aware of other aspects of reality usually hidden from us.

Are there dangers in this field? After all, as pointed out in the previous chapter, we are often up against invisible forces of evil. Isn't psychic experience just a come-on to any such forces? Of course this is often the case. Any power can be used for evil as well as for good. In our world, the telephone can be used for friendly conversation or for obscene persecution. Television can be used to show a great play or mere nonsense and violence. I have known people to show their madness through psychic delusions; but I have also known people to show instability through romantic or political delusions. Even prayer can be dangerous under certain circumstances, as we have already seen.

The wise Christian knows that evil exists and that it can attack him at his weak points. But he also learns as he grows how to keep himself under protection.

This is where the guidance of the church is so badly needed. Christians facing such experiences alone can so easily become bewildered. They may become frightened, thinking that all such psychic awareness is *per se* either a sign of insanity or demonic possession. Wise leaders could teach us the danger signs if and when they arise.

At the other extreme, a Christian, left on his own, may become unduly elated at his developing psychic ability. He may think he is becoming a prophet or saint, not realizing how widespread these experiences are. Or he may strain to have more such experiences, not realizing that such straining and forcing may really put him in danger. A little intelligent, knowledgeable leadership would help him realize, all other things being equal, that he is probably becoming neither a witch nor a saint, but is merely a growing human being who is receiving new powers.

The psychic development is in itself neither good

113

nor evil. It is an instrument come to be used in obedience to God. Psychic awareness is not a sign of sanctity, but merely a sign of growing power and sensitivity. It is a power to be committed to Christ.

In the examples that follow, I am not trying to prove by documented evidence that such things occur. There are many other books and research studies written for that purpose. I am describing some typical experiences here in order to show the wide variety of psychic experiences that growing Christians *may* have, and to discuss the most creative and safe way to handle them.

The simplest and most frequent psychic development is the telepathic exchange of thought. This potential power was discussed briefly in the chapters on prayer and again in the preceding chapter. It is the most widespread kind of extrasensory perception and, like the others, can be used for good or evil. I gave an example of its power for good earlier, when I described how one of my prayer group members suddenly thought of me at 2:00 P.M. and prayed for me even though she did not know that I was in need.

It is astonishing how rapidly this ability develops in praying individuals and groups when the power is committed to Christ and used with loving concern. Increasingly we learn that there is a reason for the sudden sharp, compelling thoughts we have of each other or of other people.

Sometimes the psychic awareness shows itself by a vivid impression or feeling. During prayer, for example, there may be a strong sensation of something similar to

114

electric power streaming into the body. Perhaps it may cause curious pressures in the head, hands, or throat. Apparently it is a genuine radiant energy, as yet un-measured by our standards, which penetrates the body-mind complex. It is the energy that is operating when we are serving as channels for healing by our interces-sory prayers. It is the vitality of God, which is changing not only ourselves, but also the people and situations around us.

This energy is around us always, of course, and, when we pray, it is operating through us, whether we are aware of it or not. We should not lay much stress on these sensations, and certainly we should not strain to experience them. But many people developing in prayer *are* genuinely and spontaneously physically aware of the power they are helping to transmit. A scientist, who is also a prayer leader, once explained it to me, "When we pray for others, our bodies and minds are changing the wavelength of heaven into the wavelength of earth."

I would recommend that these feelings, when they come, be accepted calmly as a natural enough thing, and be committed to Christ. The energy is not originat-ing with us. That is a mistake often made about and by healers. The energy comes from God and is trans-mitted through us.

Sometimes an impression comes of a vivid awareness that some "presence" is at that moment very close to us. I have lost count of the number of people who have told me about such experiences. Sometimes it seems to

115

be the presence of a person known to us who has died. Sometimes the presence is unknown to us. Usually it occurs at a time when we are not even thinking about such matters, but suddenly the impression is as sharp and clear as if the person had just walked into the room.

Should this occur, we need not become frightened. It is almost a universal experience. It doesn't mean, necessarily, that the presence is trying to get some message across. Occasionally it means that, but usually it seems to be just an expression of love and closeness. It is best simply to return a loving, companionable thought, or to pray briefly for that person's continued growth in Christ, and then to go on about our business. If there should be a sense of evil or compulsiveness about the presence, we should calmly commit him to the power and light of Christ. It cannot harm us or "possess" us unless we invite it to do so. We have nothing to fear if we are under Christ's protection.

Psychic awareness *may* develop into an ability not only to feel things, but also to see or hear things. This is called clairvoyance and clairaudience. A friend once "saw" the face of a woman she knew, brilliantly highlighted as if under floodlights. Later she learned that, at that very time, the woman had been involved in an accident and the police were using floodlights in their rescue work.

Or the clairvoyant ability may reach cross the barrier of death. A professor, sitting in his living room one night, saw standing before him a casual friend who told

116

him she had just been killed in an auto accident. He later learned, through ordinary channels, that the accident had occurred at that time.

One woman stood in the hospital room where her husband lay in a coma, and saw his smiling, living face forming in light several feet above the bed. The experience lasted several minutes. Being a sensible, matter-of-fact person, she deliberately looked several times from the unconscious body on the bed to the radiant face above it, in order to assure herself that this was not a trick of the eyes or the imagination.

Sometimes the psychically developing person may become aware of a clear, bright light, either enveloping him or other persons, or localized at some point in the room. He may become aware of varying colors around other people.

A startling psychic experience is that of temporarily leaving the physical body and standing or moving apart from it. This happens to far more people than is generally realized. It is called by several names: "projection," or "out-of-the-body-awareness," or "traveling clairvoyance." Many scientists and psychologists are quietly studying it. The experience, though surprising and even frightening to some people, is nothing harmful in itself. It is merely one sign among many that our center of consciousness is not limited to the physical body.

Usually our consciousness does manifest itself only through the five senses, because these senses serve as our means of survival and usefulness in the material world. The senses of our bodies are like the diving helmet which enables a diver to exist and work in water. But sometimes, through such experiences as "projection," we become aware that there are other levels and dimensions of reality in which we can exist.

In any case, if we find ourselves apparently apart from the body, it is not a symptom of mental instability. We should relax and quietly remind ourselves that many people have shared this experience, and we can will ourselves, without panic or strain, to join again with the physical body. The experience of death, when it comes to each of us someday, will probably be similar to this. It is probably what happens when we go to sleep or are under an anesthetic, though on those occasions we usually forget about it when we awake.

These kinds of experiences, and other similar ones, have been recorded in the scriptures and traditions of all religions. They are found in widely separated cultures all over the world. They are repeatedly mentioned in writings and depicted in art from the earliest days of recorded history. Read our own Bible, for example, with all this in mind. It is truly surprising how often such experiences as these are mentioned. Too often we have dismissed such testimony as superstitions passed on by generations of illiterates and perpetuated by dreamy neurotics.

However, it is my observation and experience that these experiences usually come not to the superstitious and the neurotic, but rather to the sensible, down-to-earth kind of people. The people who have confided in me their special awareness manage their daily lives with

118

practical good sense. They are outgoingly interested in this world and in other people. Usually they are well-educated, observant, and often professionally trained. They have a keen sense of humor. In almost every case, they are people who have grown deeply in prayer.

Nevertheless, most of them have learned to keep fairly quiet about their experiences, especially in their churches. They know the combined mockery and apprehension with which many people will respond to their experiences. Some will merely try to forget the experiences they have had. Others may drift away from their churches and join occult groups in an attempt to learn more about what has happened to them. Others, lucky enough to come across intelligent books on the subject or to meet intelligent people who have shared these experiences, meet quietly in groups for sincere inquiry and guidance.

A scientist recently attended one of these groups in their national meeting. He later wrote to me: "They all seemed very, very normal agreeable people, and not at all 'kooky.' . . . Our main impression of these personalities was that these were the sort of people we had known all our lives in our local church: quiet people, who seemed to be benignly in the background, but who somehow were always the pillars of the church."

So what can the church do to help the inquirer? It certainly should *not* start seances, or a hard sell on psychic development. Great strain or imbalance can develop if we attempt to force it. But there can be dis-

119

cussion groups, occasional interpretive sermons, and intelligent books read and recommended in order to give wise guidance to those who are interested. The facts should be brought out into the open, that psychic awareness is a normal part of life for many normal people, and is witnessed to in the Scriptures and in the lives of many holy men and women.

Above all, the church can guide the growing Christian according to the wisest dictum I ever heard concerning this matter: "For every *one* step forward you take in psychical development, take *ten* steps in moral and spiritual development."

But is there any danger that the church will attract hysterical sensation seekers if it speaks publicly of psychical matters? Of course. There is always this danger, no matter *what* we are studying: race relations, liturgical renewal, family and sex relationships, new ways of worship, or tax reform. But far more harm is done by avoidance of the subject. Heretical and fanatical fringe groups start forming when the parent church ignores any vital concern. The more ambiguous the subject— the more potentially dangerous—the greater the need for intelligent leadership.

I think at this point a word is needed on a most controversial subject that bewilders or distresses many churches: the experience of *glossolalia,* "speaking (or praying) in tongues." Actually, in my opinion, this is *not* the same thing as psychical development, but it should be mentioned here since I'm already discussing controversial matters of the spirit. Also, the growing

120

Christian should be aware of its existence, since it is a fast-growing movement in many denominations, and he *might* just possibly find himself or a close friend or a group to which he belongs participating in such an experience.

Personally, I know very little about it. I have read a few books on the subject and have talked to four knowledgeable people who use "tongues" as a means of worship. These four come from widely different backgrounds. One is a Roman Catholic priest, one is an Episcopalian schoolteacher, another is a nurse, who belongs to the Unity movement, and the fourth is a well-known leader among Pentecostalist groups. *Glossolalia* seems to these groups to be a natural way of expressing their love for God.

I have also studied the apostle Paul's sensible remarks on the subject, especially in I Corinthians 12:14. His conclusions are the wisest. This is a gift—a minor gift—given to some but not all Christians. If it comes spontaneously, it may be used for the deepening of personal and communal worship. But it should *never* be used as a test for the presence of the Holy Spirit. The best test of the Holy Spirit is whether *love* is to be found in the group. And certainly the experience of "tongues" should not be a cause for dissension in a church. We should all be much more tolerant than we are of the "varieties of gifts" among us.

Whatever experiences come our way as we grow—whether spiritual, psychological, psychic, or a mixture of the three—I think we who are growing in Christ

121

can afford to be unafraid, relaxed, open-minded, and discerning.

We can read and investigate. At the end of this book there is a reading list that includes some excellent books on the subject of parapsychology.

We can tactfully talk with other people whom we believe may have shared similar experiences.

We can join some well-balanced groups which either seek just to discover the facts, such as The American Society of Psychical Research, or seek to relate such facts to faith and theology, such as the Spiritual Frontiers Fellowship.

We can learn to accept with gratitude what comes spontaneously when resulting fruits are good, but we should avoid making a big deal out of it. It is all a very natural thing. It is merely a part of a growing sensitive ability to see a little further, communicate a little deeper, understand a little better.

Whatever "messages" come through, whether by seeing, hearing, or feeling, should be put to the guidance tests suggested earlier. Just because a message or bit of advice comes to us from another dimension that does not mean that it is necessarily right! We always have our God-given free will, our common sense, and the light of Christ (not a lesser spirit) to depend on.

As with any other power that can develop into a problem or a strength, the extrasensory ability should be committed utterly to the will, vitality, and protection of Jesus Christ. The only creative way to receive and use this power is under his unfolding guidance.

122

OUR GROWTH AND OTHER PEOPLE

So we grow. We are changing. Some things are dying in us, and other things are coming to life. Prayer is both easier and harder. Guidance is clearer. We know ourselves better now, with joy and pain. God is no longer a sentimental feeling, but now an inescapable reality. New awarenesses emerge, and the invisible levels of reality around us seem closer. With delight, suffering, and power a new being is coming to birth, just as Christ promised us.

But all this is happening within us in a world of other people. We are not off on a solitary planet. We are still members of a family. We belong to a culture. We have jobs. We are members of communities and churches.

123

We are surrounded with all kinds of people, many of whom are completely alien to this particular kind of growth and search. Perhaps some are mildly curious, indifferent, or even hostile. Some may be seeking a spiritual growth based on different premises or different criteria. Others may be unaware of any kind of spiritual growth.

What do we do? How do we relate? What is the line we take, for example, in a church that considers such questions as guidance, direct answer to prayer, and psychic awareness as irrelevant or superstitious? How do we relate to our closest friends, who are drawn to our changing selves, but are extremely indifferent to the source of that change? How about our families? Do we have a duty to witness verbally to the reason for the change in us? Is it our duty to try to guide them along the same path?

Our way *is to embrace, but not to clutch.* In fact, our ability to do this is one of the main indications that we *are* actually growing in Christ.

But at the beginning we face a constant temptation to clutch. First of all, we are likely to clutch defensively at our own beliefs and experiences, fearful lest an amused word or indifferent reaction or intellectual rebuttal somehow wither away the growing brightness we experience. It is hard at first to relax. We keep forgetting that God's light is not a feeble candle flicker that can be puffed out by any wind. Rather, it is the radiance of the eternal sun itself that we are learning

124

to see. It existed and shone long before man existed on the earth. Windows and doors may be slammed shut within us and around us, but it won't have the slightest effect on that sun.

There is a beloved, well-meaning poem which says:

> Christ has no hands but our hands
> To do his work today;
> He has no feet but our feet
> To lead men in his way . . . .[1]

It is a challenging hymn in many ways, and inspires many to greater efforts for a while. But I think the theology it expresses puts on us a burden of guilt and anxiety which, in the long run, is self-defeating. It was not because Christ was so sweet and helpless that he raised up men and women filled with his fire, living for him in joy and dying for him in song. It was because he was *not* helpless. It was because he rose in power and lives forever. It was because he freed men from the chains that bound them. It is we who are in him, really, rather than he in us. He works through us, yes. But he is independent of us. If we fail and fall, he will raise up others to take our places. Even if the whole human race should commit suicide in its folly, the burning energy of the Son of God would raise up new races and new levels of consciousness forever. He does not need us, he loves

[1] Annie Johnson Flint, "The World's Bible," Copyright. Reproduced by permission. Evangelical Publishers, Toronto, Canada.

us. He shows his love, and he changes us by letting us share in his power and his work.

The child who is made to feel that the whole household will collapse if he forgets to feed the cat or make his bed is not a happy or healthy child. To be sure, he should be taught that others depend on him for certain things, that he can help make family life easier and happier for others, and that if he neglects his work, even though it isn't fair, others will have to carry his burdens. But he should also constantly be made aware that there is a strong loving force that keeps things going, even when he has been negligent. A home built on foundations of guilt and anxious striving isn't a healthy home.

We—God's children (I don't believe at all that we are yet "man-come-of-age" or anywhere near it)— are far more challenged to works of loving concern when we are invited to experiences of creative joy than when pushed by the feeling, "It is all up to me, and everything that happens is my fault!"

I received the invitation to serve my first church in the Rocky Mountains for the summer when I had just turned twenty-one. I was far from being a wise and experienced pastor, and the little church could not afford a full-time minister. There were some in that town, especially some young people, who would hear first of Christ from me. I remember my released joy when the superintendent wrote me, "Come prepared to do your best, and leave the results in the hands of God."

Christians work best when they know the world is

held together by stronger hands than theirs. For they work then from a center of confident peace. So we do not need to clutch at God and our experience of him as we relate to the world of other people. Neither need we clutch other people! And how often do we do just that. We are so thrilled by the changes God has brought about that we grab other people in our hot little hands and try to make them share our experience.

I talked recently with a woman who was in tears of frustration because her grown children kept rebuffing her efforts to "save" them.

I still recall the hot embarrassment with which I listened to a five-minute speech in our freshman speech class in college. We had each been asked to speak on any subject of general interest while the others wrote down suggestions and comments. One earnest young man took his place in front of the class and began, "Jesus Christ can save *you!*" and then proceeded with a five-minute evangelical sermon. He was taking advantage of a captive audience, who had assembled to learn how to speak, not to listen to his religious beliefs. He was "clutching" at us.

I recall with greater embarrassment the way I kept dragging prayer into every conversation on every possible occasion, after I personally woke up to its reality. I was determined to set everybody right. I was almost convinced I had *invented* prayer. It is a wonder people didn't cross the street to escape me. Who knows—maybe they did!

G. K. Chesterton expressed his distaste for the

127

"bright beady eyes and patient smiles" of people who try to push others into their own cults.

But are we not to be witnesses? Are we not to be radiant and enthusiastic and help to open the door for others? Obviously, but it isn't our clutching hands and our breathing down his neck that will help to convert our neighbor. Such things will merely make him go in the opposite direction. And the closer the other person is to us—spouse, child, parent, best friend—the worse the effect of our "clutching" will be.

The best witness we can give is to be an increasingly radiant, happy, and fulfilled self, and to pray lovingly and joyfully and *silently* for everyone God brings our way. If others are themselves ready for this kind of growing, they will ask for the secret of our joy and our peace. Our relatives will notice gratefully that we are easier, more relaxed to live with, and may express their interest. Then we can discuss clearly and unapologetically what is happening to us through Christ.

We can let our families, friends, and church (and possibly the people who work with us) know basically where we stand in our new response to God and our new awareness of the power of prayer. To speak of this once, clearly and fully, opens the door for any exploratory desires they may have. We can keep alert to possible signals of interest or need on their part, and we can make brief references or comments about our new experiences and faith when they seem appropriate. If someone directly turns to us for counsel and help, we need not hesitate to witness.

128

"Why shouldn't I have extramarital affairs?" a young divorced woman asked me. "And please don't drag in religion. I'm not interested in it." I felt no qualms in telling her I could not possibly answer her question without reference to my religion, because my religion *was* the context for my moral decisions. But at this point I didn't feel it either necessary or appropriate to make her listen to a further witness of faith.

There have been other occasions when friends have asked for counsel on a family problem or a professional decision. When I feel that growth in prayer would be of great help to them, I tell them so, and also tell them briefly what it has done for me. If they show interest and choose to follow it up, that's fine. If they listen politely but unresponsively, then I drop that approach and discuss the problem on whatever level seems to reach them the best at that time.

Open the door, but don't push your friend through. Or to change the analogy, people must be in a state of ripeness before they are ready. Before they have reached the right time inwardly, trying to reach them is like trying to shake green apples off a tree. I have a close friend who has said (quite sincerely) at least half a dozen times, "Oh I do want to sit down with you and really talk through the questions about God, prayer, and guidance." But somehow the right time has never come for her. Through the years each time she has said this I have indicated my readiness and willingness to talk but she has not yet come to the point where she really wants to badly enough. I do not feel I should try to push this, or set a time myself, because I firmly believe that when the time is ripe for her she will let nothing stand in her way.

For years a friend tried to persuade me to read a certain book on prayer. She read parts of it out loud. She described what it had done for her. She took it out of the library for me several times. But I never got around to reading the book, though I did have a mild interest in the subject. But finally, the day came when I knew I had to read that book and read it right away. Then I went on and read everything else the author had written. Why was I ready then and not earlier when my friend had urged it on me? It was not just pure stubbornness, I hope. More likely it was one of those mysteries of slow development in the depths of the human subconscious.

When the time comes for each of us to rise up and seek the face of the Father, nothing in all creation will stop us. It is as imperious and overwhelming as the call of physical love to young men and women. No one has the right to try to push or urge someone else into that response before he is ready for it. When he is ready, nothing will stop him. He will seek out the people and books to help him. But we must learn to be sensitively alert to this awakening on the part of others, and help to guide them with prayer and sharing. They are apt to go up many blind alleys and meet bewildering situations in their first enthusiastic response to God's reality.

130

With our children we can go a bit further in witnessing to our joyous dependence on prayer. We can do this by casual conversation about it when discussing problems and people with them, and even by praying aloud in a natural, spontaneous way when they are sick or need help of some kind, or when they are being put to bed and there is an especially close feeling between parent and child. More important than set times of prayer adhered to rigidly by the family is the living presence of a parent who really does himself believe in, and live by, prayer. This is a reality which will forever be a part of children's thinking, deciding, and remembering. They may not, as they grow, choose this way for themselves for many years. Maybe not even in this life. But if and when they do, the knowledge that they have been close to at least one other person who was really changed through prayer will be of inestimable more help to them than set family devotions or theological theory.

An active young mother, who has a strong faith of her own, was trying to get her teen-agers off to church one Sunday. She was much disturbed at their recalcitrance and their resistance, and was worrying about her apparent lack of influence on them. Guilty and tense, she was wondering if she had been a good mother, a good influence. Then, as she told us later, she felt a clear command spoken within her mind, "Just give your children to me." Her guilt and anxiety seemed to drop from her. Cheerfully she told them good-bye and came on to church herself. "I realize now they belong

131

to God," she told us. "They are his children more than mine. I will keep on giving them the best that I can, and I will become a more prayerful woman myself. But I will not try to push them at God anymore." She thus gave her loved ones into God's own light, and realized anew that his love carried them even more than her own. I know her new strength and peacefulness has changed the atmosphere in her home, and provides a foundation for her children to grow and choose creatively.

When we see some friend making what seems to us a wrong or dangerous choice in life, going a long roundabout way when we are sure we know a more direct way, it is an agonizing experience for us. Then, above all, we must remember to embrace but not to clutch. We must open our hands in every possible way and lovingly let those close to us go. But we can continue to pray for them. We should not pray by making a mental blueprint of what *we* think they ought to be, but mentally envision them standing in the light of God (or picture them in his hands) and let *him* work at the kind of re-creation they need.

Prayer is action. It is the most profound action we can take on behalf of another—and the most influential. And above all, *the prayer of freedom,* which releases the person from our own possessiveness into God's hands, is the prayer that opens every door possible in their lives. It may take years for us to see the results of that kind of prayer, but it is never wasted. Its radiant energy—Christ's own fire—burns on for all eternity, in other dimensions of eternity as well as in this life. It is never too late for those we love and pray for.

A final word here. We, as growing Christians, need a good deal of healthy humility as we relate to other people. We really don't know just *what* the condition of another person's spiritual life or relationship with God is. It may be that God is leading him in a way that is incomprehensible to us but is the best way for the deep need in the person's own unique nature, considering his background and experience. It may be necessary for him at certain stages to be absorbed in activities and ways of expressing himself that are alien to us. We don't really know with other people just what have been their deep frustrations, or what energies have to be worked out, or what special gifts developed.

A young woman who had some profound mystical experiences thought this meant she was headed for a life in the ministry, or some allied profession. Everyone else thought so too, and it was a grief to many when she suddenly left the seminary and seemed for several years to drift from one job to another. For a long time she withdrew from the church altogether, and even stopped praying. We learned later that she had realized while in seminary that there were some severe emotional problems in her life, some neuroses in her relationships with others. For the time being, church surroundings and religious vocabulary made her problems worse, for they were deeply associated with some of the very roots of her problems. During the years of apparent drifting,

133

she was seeing a psychotherapist regularly, developing abilities she had ignored before, and learning more about herself and other people. Eventually she returned to prayer and then to the church with a deeper, healthier faith. She knows far more about prayer and guidance now than most people. She does not feel that she was apart from God or out of relationship with him during those years of apparently "religionless" living and seeming agnosticism. On the contrary, she was very much in his hands, being led and changed by his love.

In cases like this, where the person seems to the outsider to be drifting away from God, I think of Jesus' counsel: "If you are offering your gift at the altar, and there remember that your brother has something against you, leave your gift there before the altar and go; first be reconciled to your brother, and then come and offer your gift" (Matt. 5:23-24).

Many of those who seem to us to be moving away from what we consider to be the direct path to God may, in actuality, only be moving away from the altar to attend to some neglected part of their development. But that does not mean that they are necessarily moving away from God. They may be closer to him than they ever were before. They may have dropped the church; they may have dropped the religious vocabulary; they may have dropped even prayer and the structures of theology; but that does not mean they have dropped God. They may be aware of him, responding to him in ways that we cannot even guess.

134

This is something we cannot know about another person. We relate to him with concern yet independence, firm and unapologetic about our faith, living it radiantly, speaking of it when it is appropriate, praying always. But we relate with deep respect for the dignity of his own freedom, and with reverence for the mystery of his own growth.

When we learn the difference between the embrace and the clutch, we genuinely help to open doors to God for the people around us, perhaps for the first time.

PRAYER GROUPS—
CIRCLES OF SURRENDER

It was a heady experience, finding for the first time a group of people committed to the power of prayer. I had been investigating and learning alone for several years, and was deeply hungry for sharing and deeper experience.

This genuine hunger is an absolute essential for a healthy prayer group. It is always best that such groups form spontaneously out of mutual eagerness. There is nothing more deadly than a formally organized attempt to thrust an interest in prayer on an unprepared congregation.

Numbers do not matter. Two or three people who are genuinely interested and searching are all that is needed for a beginning. If they meet regularly, and grow in depth and experience, it is inevitable that the news will spread, and others will be drawn to their fellowship.

If it is the minister himself who is interested in such a group, he can quietly announce his concern, and invite anyone else to join him. Of course, *any* church member who belongs to such a group may, if he wishes, ask the minister to announce the meetings. It should never be pushed. The public announcements are made only to help those who are interested in such groups, and to make them feel welcome.

What, exactly, *is* a prayer group? There are certainly some very odd, exaggerated ideas about it. A healthy group is *not* one which indulges in a bathos of sentiment. It does not go in for open confession and self-analysis in depth. Its members are neither occultists nor mystical types. They do not hold themselves aloof from the active world. In the two groups to which I belong, there are men in business, publishing, teaching. There are women who are nurses, teachers, artists. One member works in a ghetto school. Another works in an atomic laboratory. The members represent about eight denominations: Congregational, Baptist, Roman Catholic, Swedenborgian, Methodist, Lutheran, Unity, Presbyterian. They represent all different shades of political opinion and theology. But the one thing they have in common is a belief in the objective, actual power of prayer which leaps over and undercuts all other differences.

137

In essence, a prayer group is a circle of surrender. Its members have evidence that the power of Christ is released, through their surrendered bodies and wills, into the suffering world. As C. S. Lewis has said, when you have two Christians together, you don't have merely twice as much Christianity, but sixteen times as much. A few years ago, when I wrote my first book on prayer, I could not yet witness to this with authority. I was still new to prayer groups, though I was already deeply convinced of the power of individual prayer. But now, four years later, I am speaking as one who has seen, not merely believed. Such groups do have a real and tremendous power.

The main symbol we hold in mind is the one used in the gospel of John: "I am the vine, you are the branches. He who abides in me, and I in him, he it is that bears much fruit. . . ." (John 15:5) Keeping this in mind guards a group against many dangers inherent in prayer groups. It reminds a group that Christ is its leader, and no one individual. It reminds the group that the power working through them is not their own, but his. It keeps a group from pride and self-sufficiency.

Every group develops its own unique personality as well as its own way of receiving and responding to Christ's presence. But there are certain growth experiences a group can expect that are similar to those of an individual. For example, a group learns to depend less on emotions and feelings, and more on the objective reality of Christ's presence and the fruits resulting from his power. It used to worry us when members of the
138

group would say, "Well, somehow tonight I didn't get as strong a feeling of God's presence and power." Or we would be unduly elated when someone would report sensations of electric power or mystical feeling. Now we realize these sensations come and go, and have very little effect on the actual results. A group learns to look at the fruits of changed lives, improved relationships, and partial or complete healings among those for whom we are praying.

Also we learn to spend very little time analyzing or diagnosing the problems of those we pray for. We are tempted, at first, to discuss the person, enumerate details, analyze reasons, outline hoped-for results. The dangers of this are obvious. It leads to gossip. It wastes time. It fixes our attention on the problem rather than on Christ's power. Worst of all, it tends to make us think that we are diagnosticians and healers. Diagnosing is not our business nor the work for which we are assembled. Not only is it irrelevant to our purpose, but it is completely outside the scope of our wisdom and power.

Some groups avoid this danger by giving only the name of the person, without mentioning the problem. Other groups find it helpful to mention briefly the particular illness or problem in order to focus concern, but they do not dwell on it.

As soon as possible, we should move away from the problem to concentrate on the Christ, who is working on that problem. This can be done through silent meditation, or through brief vocal prayers offered by the

139

leader or one of the members. Or there can be a combination of silent praying and spontaneous vocal praying. No one should be made to feel he has to speak aloud each evening. Personally, I'm not in favor of the custom of going around the circle, with each member expected to lead in prayer.

Some groups keep a list of names to pray for. If this is done, there should be some follow-up on the names from time to time, so the list does not get too long or unwieldy as the weeks go on. Our own group keeps no list written but asks for names each time we meet. If there are many names on one particular evening, we have a temporary list for that evening alone. And we always ask God to put into our minds the names of those who most need prayer at that time.

Whatever the method used, the group learns to place the *whole* person and problem into the hands of Christ. We see only the surface symptoms, the illness, the addiction, the marriage conflict. But God sees the roots of the trouble. Healing may have to begin far below the surface, and it may be a long time before we see results, so we should be neither impatient nor discouraged. The slow but deep work going on in a person with profound problems may be far more of a miracle than a swift and spectacular change.

The basic reason we exist at all as a prayer group is to surrender our combined powers to Christ and hold the unseen as well as the visible problems of each person in the healing light. We grow in confidence— not in ourselves, but in this light. I have never yet seen

140

a situation in which there was not at least some change and improvement when a surrendered group held it persistently in this light. And it is not because God is doing us a favor. One of the main points of this book which can't be repeated too often, is that intercessory prayer is not begging God, it is cooperating with God. It is opening ourselves to that which is already his nature—healing, creative love.

One of my prayer group members once said thoughtfully that when we pray we are helping create an atmosphere, much as trees help create oxygen, which enables others to live more fully, breathe more deeply, make better choices, and open themselves to God.

Another friend helpfully pointed out that when we pray for others we bring them to Christ for renewal, much as the veins in the body bring the tired, impure blood to the heart for renewal.

A prayer group learns to grow in discipline. It not only learns to refrain from gossip and diagnosis and personal pride, but it also learns to remain primarily a working group. A prayer group comes together for work, not for social purposes or discussions. Of course, there should be a little time for the expression of warm concern and fellowship. And there should be a brief time to report on the progress or continued need of those who have been prayed for, and to share aspects of the members' own growing. There is room for humor, too. A minister once walked by one of the prayer group rooms and later asked, "Are you sure that was a prayer group going on in there? I heard such shouts of laughter,

141

I thought some other group was meeting!" Indeed, as we grow, we find there is infinitely more to laugh at than to weep about. And what's more, we grow in the joy, humility, and irony with which we express our laughter. But after the brief, warm sharing, a group should swiftly and purposefully move on to their work of exposing themselves to the power of Christ and serving as his channels.

Starting and ending promptly are among the disciplines learned. Groups that allow meetings to go on and on for hours into the night lose much of their fire and enthusiasm, and even some members after a few months. It is only fair to say here that there are some leaders who do not at all agree with me on this point. They feel that to set a firm time limit on a prayer group meeting is to limit its spontaneity and the freedom of the Holy Spirit. I realize that rigidity on this point is wrong. Sometimes it is obvious that a group wishes to stay longer, praying and talking together, and at such times, of course, they should. But it still seems to me that, if a group of busy people plan to do the work of group prayer together for several years, it is better to have time limits set that they can count on and plan around. It is better for steady, healthy growing in the spirit to meet regularly for forty-five minutes or an hour each week, than to meet for four hours one week and none the next. Our own group has not encouraged the serving of refreshments even when we meet in private homes, for the same reason. There are many groups (and they are fine ones) that meet for sociability and

142

discussion. But there are relatively few groups that meet for the work of prayer alone.

A healthy group learns that its members should not lean on each other too much. There should be trust and concern of course, but not dependence. As in all our relationships, we should embrace but not clutch. Prayer group members do not have to be best friends. It may turn out that one finds a good friend in a prayer group, but it does not necessarily happen. Friendships are formed when two people find they have much in common; but in a prayer group, the members may have very little in common except their belief in the power of prayer. We should pray for each other frequently, for we are involved in the same ministry. We should report to each other when a special need for prayer arises between meetings. But we don't have to share all our thoughts and actions.

Many members of my groups have very little in common with me. I know little about their personal lives. But this does not matter, because we trust each other and turn to each other as dependable colleagues in this kind of work. We receive our strength from the same Lord, and when the meetings are over we go our separate ways with warm good-byes for each other.

It is another matter if actual dislike or repulsion should arise between some members. I have occasionally been in groups where an undercurrent of dislike was chronic between two or three people. That situation can quickly destroy the vitality of a group. It is a serious obstacle between the members and the energy

143

of Christ. If real antagonism is growing in us toward another member, we have the choice of going to another group or, better yet, of relinquishing the hostile feeling to Christ and asking him to deal with it.

Hypocrisy or enmity need not grow just because the members of a group disagree on political or social issues. Here in Berkeley we are constantly in the midst of many conflicting events, such as campus strikes, confrontations, and demonstrations for all kinds of purposes. We in the prayer group are by no means of one mind about these questions. We would probably not agree on solutions, no matter how long we talked. Some of our members are extremely liberal, others are definitely conservative. But we know this need not make the slightest difference in our work as prayer partners. We *all* agree that God is far greater than our own individual opinions. We work for our opinions with vigor and integrity, but when we meet in prayer, we surrender all issues to his sovereignty, and give ourselves over as channels for *his* solutions.

What about the problem of people who come to a prayer group out of personal need rather than out of their desire to give? What about the occasional person who is more than a little neurotic, and tries to turn the group into his own psychotherapy session? This is a sticky problem. We know, if we are under guidance, that this person has been sent to us for a reason. We know as Christ's men and women that His guidance leads us to loving openness and helpfulness. At the

144

same time, we know that, if this person is allowed to dominate the scene and take over with his own needs, the group purpose can disintegrate.

There are several ways of handling this. The member can be lovingly received, listened to, counseled, and prayed for, during at least *part* of each session. But after a while the leader must gently but firmly remind everyone that this is not primarily a discussion group, but a working group, and thus lead them back to their job of praying for others rather than talking about themselves. This can be done with kindly tact, but it must also be done with unapologetic strength. A group need not fear that they are selfish or heartless if they are quite firm about not allowing any one person to take over all the time with his troubles. There are other existent groups whose purpose is that of mutual psychotherapy.

An intercessory prayer group has other work to do. And actually this may be exactly the thing that will help the dependent member the most! Bit by bit he may get the point of why this group exists. He may slowly learn to look to the objective reality of prayer and the Christ of prayer as more helpful to him than endless airing of his emotional troubles to the others. I have seen some really astounding changes of this kind. It is well for the other members of the group to remember that he, the apparently dependent member, is also being used by Christ to transmit the same power that works through them. He is probably being used far

145

more than we realize, as he struggles to let Christ take over his problems. The group may really need this suffering member more than they know.

Occasionally, each of us will become temporarily a dependent member. There are times when we feel overwhelmed with some problem—physical or emotional. It is best to tell the group about it briefly, ask for their prayers, and gratefully accept their loving concern. There is nothing to be ashamed of. It is only good sense. None of us are surprised when, occasionally, one of our strongest members sinks into his chair with a tired smile and says, "I am going to have to commit myself to the group tonight for prayer support. I am sunk, frankly." Sometimes they tell us why, sometimes they don't. It doesn't matter. We express our compassion, and pray for that member in due course as matter-of-factly as we pray for anyone else.

It is an important growth to learn not to depend too much on the leader. Some groups form spontaneously without anyone taking a leadership role, and with everyone taking turns. But sometimes a group forms around an enthusiastic—even charismatic—person. There is nothing innately wrong about that. The leader need not be self-conscious about it or overwhelmed with apologetic humility. He can be as strong and enthusiastic and overflowing as he pleases. But he mustn't become a group psychiatrist, Father Superior, or mother-substitute. He can share his thoughts, give his advice when asked, guide and lead when it seems necessary. But he and the others must remember that he is human, and being human he will sometimes surprise and disappoint his group. Sometimes he will get sick or tired. Sometimes he may give the wrong advice. Sometimes he will be tactless. A leader should be himself, without apology, but be his *whole* self—not just his best and strongest self. He shouldn't wear a disguise with his group or pretend he is feeling healthier and more loving than he actually is. He should ask for prayers just as freely and frankly as anyone else. He can share his latest insight with enthusiasm, but also share the fact that he is baffled by a problem. Above all, he must constantly point out (to himself as much as the others) that Jesus Christ is the only real leader of any group, and the only infallible one.

An amusing and extreme example of leader idolatry was expressed recently with all sincerity by a young woman I was talking with. She had been describing her beloved group leader with deep enthusiasm. "But she *does* admit that she sometimes makes mistakes, doesn't she?" I asked cautiously. "Oh, of course," the young woman answered artlessly. "She's the first to admit that she is human and makes mistakes. But, of course, her *teachings* are never wrong!"

Whether the leader claimed this for herself, or whether her group claimed it for her, I could only pray, "God help them!"

As a group grows in maturity and wisdom, it learns that it is not an occult clique of "those in the know," far advanced in the realm of the Spirit, leaving behind

147

those other poor benighted church members who know nothing of the mysteries of prayer! Of all repulsive forms a group can take, this is the worst. Of course, a group can sometimes be quite innocent of this attitude, and the other church members *think* this is the way they are feeling. Only time, results, and the simple unaffectedness of the group members will allay this suspicion. Group members will be wise not to chatter too much about their group and its important function to other church people. They can refer to it occasionally in a matter-of-fact way as a vital part of church life, but they need not act as if they were condescending to the "spiritual kindergarten" of the rest of the church. Always remember the warning given in the last chapter of about the "bright beady eyes and patient smiles"!

It is healthy to remember—we who are called to group prayer—that many people far beyond us in prayer experience do not have the vocation of this kind of group ministry. They pray only as individuals, and often with great power. We cannot tell positively, as we look around us at the people in the pews and working on the committees, just who among them may be literally spiritual giants whose silent prayer helps hold us all together.

A prayer group does indeed serve as a pinch of hidden yeast in the dough. The whole life and direction of a church can be powerfully affected by the existence of a committed praying group who constantly hold the ministers, the committees, the teachers, the trustees and deacons, and the choir (by name) in the light of

Christ. A church without any such group is a church in trouble. I say this without any qualification.

But the group must remember that yeast is useless unless it is *in* the dough. Whether they meet in a church or in a private home, whether they are formed out of only one denomination or many, they exist to serve the community as well as the world. The basis of all such groups is the Church Universal. We are never out of it. Even if we were alone in the wilderness we would still be Christ's men, responsible to all fellow-lovers of Christ, uplifting them in prayer, and being uplifted by them. There is something wrong and unhealthy about a prayer group which has detached itself, broken off, and is no longer responsible to a larger community of faith.

Finally, a healthy prayer group will grow in flexibility and willingness to change. Just as an individual can make an idol of any one method or insight and thus stop growing, so can a group. The very method that helped make them originally a group of power can be the very thing that drains away their power and turns them into petrified wood. This, of course, is the whole history of denominationalism in the Christian church. A group will rise, on fire, radiant with the freshness of the living Christ. The members will find a certain method of expressing their love for Christ and their fellow-men that serves them well. Then they stick rigidly to that method of worship and service though both the times and their needs have changed. This means that they are no longer in the hands of the living Christ, but

149

have attached themselves to an idol. Growth has stopped, and petrifaction or rot has set in. Not only have they become unfree, but they then seek in their growing hunger to impose their rigid structure on others. And they wonder sadly or angrily why others resist them, and why the joy and freshness have gone out of the organization.

It is our pathetic, ruthless history. It is the meaning behind the strange prayer in our liturgies: "Take not thy Holy Spirit from us." God never removes his love and forgiveness. But the power of his living Christ will turn to other channels when one is blocked against him— even though that channel has been open to him in the past.

We must constantly pray to be kept flexible, limber in his hands, aware of new methods, aware of new needs. Christ alone, no method, is "the same, yesterday, today, and forever."

THE PARADOX OF GROWING

You are here. You are actually here. You are not words, words, words. You are not things, things, things, nor even prayer which leads us to You, to the open door that You have never allowed to be closed to us. You are not an idea or an intellectual concept difficult to figure out nor a magic formula, nor a dread destiny which we must propitiate. You are the Christ who walked the roads as we do. You are the Holy Spirit that descended on the apostles. You are *here*.[1]

In this prayer to the living Christ, we find the ultimate secret of Christian vitality. We find the secret of

---

[1] Adela Rogers St. Johns, *Tell No Man* (New York: Doubleday & Co., 1966), p. 255.

151

the power that makes us grow. *Christianity is a marriage feast.* The riot of color in stained glass, the trumpets in church on Easter morning, the unique warm power in the Christian's life, all "the singing and the gold"—all these arise from an actual transaction between our personality and the personality of Christ. Those Christians whose radiance has cast out fear and destroyed enslavement are those Christians who are most keenly aware that their union with Christ is with a risen, living person. Married to his radiance, endowed with his energy, they move as spearheads into the dark fields of distorted and demonic energy.

Once we forget this, and turn our faith into a system of morality or a philosophical theory, most of our unique vitality goes down the drain. It is not a dead creed or a respectable ethic we are celebrating. It is a marriage feast!

Once there was a man, Jesus Christ, who was utterly one with God. And there is *still* this man, who is utterly one with God! The implications of this are boundless.

And here is our paradox. We have seen the need for our real growing and changing. We have been promised by Christ that he will change us. What's more, we begin, as we pray, to see the changes actually beginning. But we must remind each other always that change and growth are brought about most swiftly when we don't keep our eyes on them, but on the Christ who brings them.

I am not exactly saying about this book, "Now that you've read it, forget it." But I am saying something

152

fairly close. The best way to impede growth is to keep measuring it and worrying about it.

I remember an evening spent with a highly-educated, newly-married young couple. Their conversation the whole evening was larded with extreme self-consciousness about the state of their relationship. He would make a remark. She would look arch and knowing. He would say, "Ah, yes. I see that when I said that I was really projecting on *you* the basic hostility I feel for myself!" "Yes," she would answer gravely. "I wondered when you would realize that." On and on it went. Endless mutual analysis and self-analysis. They couldn't forget that they were two people in a *relationship*. Apparently no one else before had ever been in a *relationship*. They couldn't take their anxious eyes off the exact state of that relationship for a minute.

The captive audience to this dialogue were invited to join them in this digging up and replanting of roots. What a relief it was finally to get out of that hothouse of self-awareness and go back to people who were just spontaneously being themselves, willing to make occasional mistakes.

We see this anxious mutual reviewing often going on in prayer or discussion groups. We see it in parents with their first child. We see it when boys and girls first begin to charm each other. Doctors see it when patients first wake up to the state of their health. Too much of the wondering "How'm I doing? How'm I doing?" is the death of charm, health, influence, and genuine change. A painter recently told me, "You

153

mustn't be too analytically concerned when in the actual process of painting. Visualize it ahead of time, step back occasionally and get the effect, but when the brush is in the hand—let's go!"

Obviously a certain amount of measuring and reviewing is not only healthy but necessary. Intelligent information about general patterns of growth, the types of results that can be expected, and the symptoms of decay or illness is needed. That is why I wrote this book. Christians must know the facts and experiences of the change they will experience through Christ. But several of my friends cringed a bit when I told them I was writing about personal growth in Christ (I used the heavy word "sanctification," which made them look even sicker), because immediately they envisioned all the harm a book like that can do if it gets too solemn or anxious.

I hesitated before writing the book because I, too, knew what a travesty of Christian joy it would be if, each day, my readers began to wonder such things as, "How does my spiritual condition *today* compare with my spiritual condition *yesterday?*"; "Are people noticing a change in me yet?"; "I haven't experienced the 'dark night of the soul' yet. I wonder when it's going to hit!"; or "When do I start getting all those psychic experiences she talks about?". Anyone who has the impertinence to write a book like this must realize that it can very easily lay a load of anxiety on readers who already are carrying around far too heavy a load of guilt and worry.

But I found a safeguard in a saying of that tough and

robust personality St. Theresa of Lisieux, that I commend to every reader as he turns his attention to the patterns and fruits of his Christian growing: *"Work not to become saints, but rather to give joy to God."*

Paste this saying in your hat. Stick it on the mirror. Tape it to the kitchen sink or the steering wheel. Carry it in your mind and heart wherever you go, and all will be well with you in your growing.

The Christian discipline and the Christian development is much more like a dance than like gymnastics. We learn the steps and the beat, our muscles grow more limber and more tough, the parts of the body coordinate. But underlying the muscular development is the joy, the fellowship, the gladness, and the grace. Think about that theological concept of the grace of God, which lifts from us the burden and the anxious striving. It is his grace, and our responsive gracefulness, which empower us to undertake a life of righteousness with lightness of heart.

God will lead the dance with the righteous . . . and they will dance before him with vigor, and they will point with the finger and say: "This God is our God forever and ever; He will lead us beyond death; in two worlds he will lead us, in this world and the world to come." [2]

[2] *A Rabbinic Anthology.* Arr. C. G. Montefiore and H. Loewe. Jewish Publication.

155

SUGGESTED READING

CHRISTIAN BELIEF AND LIVING

Berger, Peter L. *A Rumor of Angels.* Garden City, N.Y.
    Doubleday & Co., 1969.

Capon, Robert F. *Bed and Board.* New York: Simon &
    Schuster, 1965.

Duncombe, David. *The Shape of the Christian Life.*
    Nashville: Abingdon Press, 1969.

Lewis, C. S. *Mere Christianity.* New York: The Macmil-
    lan Co., 1960.

————. *The Four Loves.* London: Geoffrey Bles, 1960.

Malenia, Fae. *The Quantity of a Hazel Nut.* New York:
    Alfred A. Knopf, 1968.

Marshall, Catherine. *Beyond Our Selves.* New York:
    Avon Books, 1961.

Merton, Thomas. *The New Man.* New York: Farrar,
    Straus & Giroux, 1963.

O'Connor, Elizabeth. *Journey Inward, Journey Out-
    ward.* New York: Harper & Row, 1968.

Phillips, Dorothy B., ed. *The Choice Is Always Ours.*
    New York: Harper & Row, 1960.

Sanford, Agnes. *Behold Your God.* St. Paul, Minn.:
    Macalester Park, 1958.

Smith, Hannah W. *The Christian's Secret of a Happy
    Life.* New York: Grosset & Dunlap, 1968.

Tournier, Paul. *The Adventure of Living.* New York:
    Harper & Row, 1965.

157

————. *The Meaning of Persons.* New York: Harper & Row, 1957.

Weatherhead, Leslie D. *The Christian Agnostic.* Nashville: Abingdon Press, 1965.

PRAYER

Boyd, Malcolm. *Are You Running with Me, Jesus?* New York: Holt, Rinehart, and Winston, 1968.

Brandt, Leslie. *Good Lord, Where Are You?* St. Louis: Concordia Publishing House, 1967.

Kelly, Thomas. *A Testament of Devotion.* New York: Harcourt, Brace & World, 1964.

Magee, John. *Reality and Prayer.* New York: Harper & Row, 1957.

Parker, William R., Johns, E. St. Elaine. *Prayer Can Change Your Life.* Englewood Cliffs, N.J.: Prentice-Hall, 1957.

Wuellner, Flora S. *Prayer and the Living Christ.* Nashville: Abingdon Press, 1969.

PARAPSYCHOLOGY AND PSYCHICAL RESEARCH

Journal of The American Society for Psychical Research. 5 West 73rd St., New York, N.Y.

Spiritual Frontiers Fellowship Quarterly Journal. 800 Custer Ave., Evanston, Ill.

Banks, Frances. *Frontiers of Revelation.* London: Max Parrish, 1962.

Hart, Hornell. *The Enigma of Survival.* London: Rider & Co. 1959.

Heywood, Rosalind. *Beyond the Reach of Sense.* New York: E. P. Dutton, 1961.

Johnson, Raynor. *The Imprisoned Splendour.* New York: Citadel Press, 1951.

Rhine, Joseph B. *The Reach of the Mind.* New York: Apollo, 1961.

Steinour, Harold. *Exploring the Unseen World.* New York: Citadel Press, 1951.

Tyrell, G. N. M. *The Personality of Man.* Baltimore: Penguin Books, 1947.

White, Stewart Edward. *The Unobstructed Universe.* New York: E. P. Dutton, 1940.

FICTION PERTAINING TO SPIRITUAL GROWTH

Lewis, C. S. *The Great Divorce.* New York: The Macmillan Co., 1946.

————. *Perelandra.* New York: The Macmillan Co., 1944.

————. *Till We Have Faces: A Myth Retold.* New York: Harcourt, Brace & World, 1956.

Salinger, J. D. *Franny and Zooey.* Boston: Little, Brown, 1961.

St. Johns, Adela Rogers. *Tell No Man.* Garden City, New York: Doubleday & Co., 1966.

Williams, Charles. *All Hallows Eve.* New York: Farrar, Straus, & Co., 1948.

————. *Descent Into Hell.* Grand Rapids: William B. Eerdmans Co., 1949.

Date Due

M.

DISCARDED
BY
STANLEY LIBRARY
FERRUM COLLEGE